DOCTOR AT THE BAR

DOCTOR AT THE BAR

by

Cyril F. Baron

JOHNSON PUBLICATIONS LIMITED

Published 1977

SBN 85307 171 3

Published by Johnson Publications Limited,
11/14 Stanhope Mews West, London, S.W.7
and printed by Unwin Brothers Limited
The Gresham Press, Old Woking, Surrey

Contents

Chapter 1

The Beginning

It has been said by somebody that all autobiographical reminiscence is arrogant – unless one has something particularly of importance or interest to say. As to that I must leave any who read this book to judge, and if I am thought to have been too self-important I apologise. But it has seemed to me that some recollections of a life divided, as it were, between the two professions of medicine and the law might prove to be worth putting into print. These recollections, after all, might interest even the layman.

It was Bernard Shaw who said in *The Doctor's Dilemma* that all professions were conspiracies against the laity, and as, in a sense, a doubly-dyed conspirator, I may be forgiven for offering some personal recollections of both professions. It was a layman who is reported to have said, in answer to the question of which of the two professions he considered the more important that he felt, on balance, that the law was the more important; because, he added, that if a doctor advised him to take a long holiday he might disregard the advice; but if a lawyer advised him to leave the country, he would not hesitate.

Rather on the same level is the reflection that when leading counsel has opened his case to the court, he turns to his junior behind him and says: "Have I left anything out?" Whereas a careful surgeon, before closing the incision in his patient might be well advised to ask: "Have I left anything in?"

Since my retirement a number of friends have suggested that I should put into writing an account of my experiences and adventures. I have usually replied that if I were to do that, I would be inundated with claims for libel; but I hope that my apprenticeship in libel chambers will have prevented this unhappy result.

My wife deserves my deep gratitude for her patient toleration of my strangeness of behaviour during the conception, gestation, and birth of this book. It is probably unnecessary for me to say (but I shall still say it) that the opinions which I express in it are my own, and not those of anyone else.

It was decided, quite early in my life, that I was to be a doctor. I ought to say at once that this was not a decision in which I took any part. Rather was it, as it were, a family decision. This must have rested to some extent upon the apparent facility with which I dealt with examination papers. (Lest I should be thought to be presumptuous I hasten to add that this did not rest upon any excessive development of my cerebral hemispheres, but rather on the fortunate possession of a kind of photographic memory, which has always stood me in good stead).

Accordingly in 1919 at the mature age of sixteen, I enrolled as a medical student at University College, London. (In fact the classes were identical with those taken by science students in chemistry, physics, botany and zoology). Many of my fellow students were much older than I was; in fact the majority were ex-service men recently demobilised after the war of 1914–1918, and whose courses were being paid for by a grateful government. Some were even older than that. I remember among them Adrian Stephen and his wife Karen Stephen (both later to qualify and to become psychiatrists). Adrian Stephen was brother to Virginia Woolf and himself was connected with what was known as the "Bloomsbury Set".

The perhaps otherwise staid atmosphere of University College was enlivened by the presence in the same building of the Slade School of Art, whose students – deservedly or not I do not know – were generally regarded as being rather "fast";

this, in my callow and juvenile mind, was somehow associated with their practice of making paintings of ladies "in the altogether". The principal of the Slade School was in fact a man originally a surgeon – Professor Tonks. The Slade students were colourful and wore unusual and attractive clothes; they used to drape themselves decoratively on the steps of the college.

I became familiar with the anatomies of the earthworm, the dogfish, the frog and the rabbit. I must confess that I was never able to muster much enthusiasm for botany, and must have come as close to failure in that subject when the examination took place at the end of the year as possible.

But I did pass in all the necessary subjects. There then followed a long vacation, it seemed to me unnecessarily long, of three months. During this time I became a student member of the Middle Temple, and sat for one subject in what was then Part One of the Bar examinations. I was introduced into an entirely new world. I was fascinated and deeply impressed when "eating dinners" in Middle Temple Hall where once Queen Elizabeth the First had dined – the procession into and out of Hall before and after dinner of the Benchers and their guests (one of them being on one occasion Lord Birkenhead, the Lord Chancellor).

But this was only the beginning of my association with the law, and a very early and tentative one at that, and in due course I proceeded to my second medical year's subjects of anatomy, physiology and pharmacology. In these our instructors were distinguished in their own fields. In anatomy we received lectures from Professor (later Sir) Grafton Elliot Smith. His lectures were on a very high academic level, and dealt mostly with his favourite subject – the evolution and structure of the human brain. One always felt that, fascinating as his lectures were, most of the material would not help us to pass our humdrum examinations.

Then there was Jack (later Sir Jack) Drummond who lectured to us on biology and the chemistry of food. Sadly, he and his wife were later to become the victims of the still unsolved murder which took place when they were touring in

France. There were Professors Starling and Bayliss, both physiologists of international fame, who also lectured to us.

During my work in the dissecting room, at one time I shared the dissection of an arm with an ex-service student, who had the good fortune to live in an attractive country district, from which he travelled to London every day. It is perhaps not surprising that on one fine day early in the year I received a telegram from him in these words: "Spring calls. Cannot work." And he did not, and I was left to pursue my anatomical studies alone, at any rate for that day.

Another interesting character was an Indian student with extremely wealthy parents. This gentleman did very little work as a student, but savoured the fleshpots of London with great gusto, and took care that his parents continued to supply him with adequate funds. The story which ought to have been true of him, but was possibly true of some other student, runs something like this. Having exhausted all the reasonable reasons for having money sent to him – living expenses, fees, new microscope, new instruments and so on, this inventive man eventually sent a telegram to his parents in India, saying: "Please send five hundred pounds immediately. Urgently need new pair of Fallopian Tubes." For the benefit of those who do not know, I should add that the Fallopian Tubes form part of the female genital anatomy. A possibly equally accurate account is that of the medical student who had been bequeathed by a wealthy aunt a handsome income "so long as he remained a "medical student". This student, who in any event found examinations rather difficult, made sure that he remained a student – unqualified – for many years, and enjoyed a very good standard of living.

At the end of my third year, having completed the necessary examinations in anatomy, physiology, and pharmacology, I made what was perhaps a curious decision, and certainly not a usual one. Most students at that stage automatically went "across the road" to University College Hospital for their clinical studies. This, in fact was by no means an obligatory move, although such a move had, obviously, to be made towards some hospital medical school. It occurred to me that there were other, and equally famous and prestigious medical schools in London, and I eventually decided to go to St. Bartholomew's Hospital in the City of London, where I was warmly accepted. It is said that in professional circles there is some magic mystique or cachet attaching to a doctor who is a Bart's man. Possibly something of this sort was in my mind; could a reason have been (although I am not, and was not, a misogynist), that Bart's accepted only male students, whereas University College Hospital did not mind which sex one belonged to?

After an interview with the Dean of the Medical School at Bart's I was accepted as a student, and arrangements were made for my first appointment as clerk to one of the physicians. A telephone call from the Dean's office established that the great man was at that very moment in one of his wards and I was taken over to see him. I found him sitting at the bedside of one of his women patients whose somewhat distended abdomen he was diligently inspecting. Straightening himself up he shook me warmly by the hand and resumed his inspection. I was irresistibly reminded of Sir Luke Fildes' painting, "The Doctor", which depicts the doctor sitting by the bedside of a sick child. It was not until several days later that it occurred to my cynical mind that in both cases the doctor had no very clear idea what was wrong with his patient. In those days, of course, the practice of medicine had not made the skilled technological advances which it has achieved to-day. There were no antibiotics, no sulphonamide drugs; the interpretation of the electrocardiogram was in its infancy, and the use of insulin for the treatment of diabetes was only beginning to be evolved. The number of effective remedies at hand for the use of the physician were few: morphia, digitalis, quinine and others. The art of X-Ray diagnosis was still far removed from the skills of today. Blood transfusion did not exist. The personality of the physician, as to some extent even now, determined the effectiveness of the treatment.

My time at hospital was fairly fully occupied. Promptly at half past one each day, the consultant for whose "firm" one was working would appear at the fountain in the central hospital square, having just dismounted from his Rolls or Daimler, and most immaculately clothed in morning coat, striped trousers, and top hat. One would go round the wards with him. At other times one was free to go the rounds with other consultants. At this particular period, one of the most eminent physicians in London was Sir Thomas (later Lord) Horder, and I made a practice of attending his rounds in addition to those of the physician to whom I was attached. During one of Sir Thomas's rounds he came to an empty bed; there was a whispered conversation between him and the ward sister, and he then proceeded to the next bed which was occupied. It was all too clear what had happened, I thought. He was no better than the others; his patients sometimes died. My confidence evaporated, and in my naivety I ceased to go on Sir Thomas's rounds.

A popular series of lectures at Bart's was that on venereal diseases. These lectures were given by Kenneth Walker, a distinguished genito-urinary surgeon, who had a dry and mordant sense of humour. Many students gave themselves the pleasure of going to the same lectures year after year in order to enjoy the Rabelaisian stories appropriate to the subject, and which Walker told so well.

One was of the country practitioner (perhaps an old Bart's man) who sent to the pathological laboratory a specimen taken from the vagina of a female patient with the request that this should be examined for the presence of gonococci (the causal organisms of gonorrhea). "My colleagues and I", said Walker "made a thorough search for these organisms, but found none. We sent a report to the doctor saying: 'No gonococci seen, but advise further specimen'. After a few days a second specimen arrived. This specimen was swarming with gonococci. We sent a report to the doctor saying 'Second specimen swarming with gonococci'. By return there came the doctor's reply: 'Your second report arrived too late. The second specimen was from my own urethra'."

Another "outing" which we used to make from the hospital for specialised instruction was to Bethlem Royal Hospital – the original prototype for the well-known "Bedlam". This was a lunatic asylum in South London presided over by the consultant physician in psychological medicine; he fitted perfectly the picture of the Harley Street consultant, immaculately tailored. Amid Hogarthian scenes of demented patients, he would point out to us specific examples of particular types of mental disease.

A distinguished member of the staff was Sir Bernard Spilsbury, of whom one could almost say that no murder trial was complete without his evidence; in the world of forensic medicine he stood head and shoulders above his contemporaries; he was the ideal witness, giving his evidence in a cool, quiet, but deadly manner (certainly often so as far as the prisoner was concerned).

I remember very well the day on which Spilsbury's name had appeared in the morning newspapers in the Honours List, a knighthood having been conferred upon him. At lunchtime in the medical school refectory, he made his way to the top table where the staff lunched, amid a clamour of hand-clapping, feet-stamping, and loud cheering. Having at first taken his seat amid this tumult, he then, later, rose to his feet and said: "Thank you, gentlemen, I am more sinned against than sinning".

It was Sir Bernard Spilsbury, it will be recalled, who played a leading role later during the Second World War in the plan by which a body was placed in the sea off the Spanish coast – the body carrying false documents which gave a false date and place for the invasion of Europe by the Allied forces. The body was provided by courtesy of Bentley (later Sir Bentley) Purchase, the North London Coroner with whom Spilsbury worked closely. The episode has been very ably described by Ewen Montagu in his book: *The Man who Never Was*. When this cloak-and-dagger scheme was being evolved and discussed, Spilsbury was asked whether it would not be clear to a Spanish pathologist that the body had not drowned, but was already dead before being put into the sea. Spilsbury, who evidently had his own views on Spanish pathological skill, replied that the Spaniards would never notice it. He was, in the event, absolutely right, and the plan succeeded perfectly in misleading the Axis.

At Bart's I competed for the Wix Prize. Since I was awarded this prize by the examiners I can only conclude that there were few, if any, other entrants or competitors. The award was to be made for an essay on *The life and works of Thomas Glisson.* Dr. Glisson was the man who first described and identified the covering of the liver, which was therefore afterwards known as Glisson's capsule. In order that the adjudicators of the essay should not know the identity of each competitor, we were asked to identify our entries only by a motto. The motto I chose was *Ars longa, vita brevis,* the sound of which evoked some ribald comments from some of my fellow students who did not have the advantage of a classical education.

I discovered that there was a great deal of free entertainment available in London; for example, almost opposite the hospital at the Old Bailey. There was a convention whereby the attendants at the court would admit anybody muttering the words: "Bart's student". In my case the similarly sounding words "Bar student" provided an equally effective "Open Sesame".

The High Court in the Strand provided much instruction and education. There were some fascinating characters to be observed there. Mr. Justice Rigby Swift had a rich North-country accent which it is quite impossible to reproduce on paper. He was once trying a personal injury case in which the plaintiff, a young girl, sustained damage to her eyes which gave her diplopia, or double vision. She was being represented by Sir Patrick Hastings, then at the height of his career, and often appearing, or attempting to appear, in several cases in different courts at the same time. There came the inevitable moment when Hastings' clerk pulled at his gown, indicating that he was wanted in another court. Whereupon Swift addressed the plaintiff, who was then in the witness box. Swift said: "Miss—, you complain that you see two of everything?" "Yes, my lord." "Do you see two of Sir Patrick Hastings?" "Yes, my lord." "Then you had better watch them very carefully, because one of them is going out of court."

There was an Italian film – *Bigamia,* which showed precisely this sort of situation. Vittorio de Sica, as the fashionable Roman advocate, bursts into a bigamy hearing, and puts damaging questions to his own witness in the mistaken belief that he has been instructed by the other side.

I do not know how particular cases were then, or are now allocated to individual judges in the High Court, but it seemed to happen that many *causes celebres* found their way into Rigby Swift's court. By the very nature of these cases, this frequently meant that Sir Patrick Hastings on the one side would be opposed by Norman Birkett on the other.

Swift, presiding over the proceedings in his rotund, florid, and almost avuncular style, seemed to have a built-in gastric mechanism by which his stomach (or possibly his thirst) would prompt him almost exactly at one o'clock each day to intervene and say: "Sir Patrick – and Mr. Norman Birkett – would this be a convenient moment to adjourn?" Both these distinguished gentlemen – no doubt prompted by the same basic need for refreshment – would hasten to accept his lordship's suggestion.

After lunch, Swift would return to the Bench looking rather more florid and better nourished than before; he would listen to the evidence while contemplatively sucking the top end of his quill pen, the lower end of which was immersed in the inkwell; it used to be maliciously suggested that the inkwell contained not ink, but whisky, but I am sure that this was not so.

There was a case before Swift about the sale of a fur coat. In order to assist his lordship an attractive mannequin (or, as I suppose she would now be called, a model) walked up and down on the Bench wearing the coat. This was no doubt a not unwelcome addition to the judge's working day. Counsel continued his argument about the coat, and then noticing Swift's almost excessive and masculine interest in the mannequin said: "Your lordship IS looking at the *COAT*?"

In another case in which an attractive and female member of the Bar – then a much rarer phenomenon than it now is – was engaged, there was a discussion at the end of the case as to who should pay the costs. Swift turned to the lady, and said: "What do you say, Miss—?" "Well, my lord" she replied, "I'm in your lordship's hands," to which Swift is reported to have said: "I wish you were."

I never heard F. E. Smith (later Lord Birkenhead) in court, but the stories of his powerful and fearless advocacy are legendary and legion. In one case he is said to have been putting his case at great length and in great detail to the judge. The judge began to show signs of increasing restlessness and impatience. He eventually interrupted, and said: "You know, Mr Smith, all that you say makes me no wiser." "No, my lord." immediately said Smith, "but your lordship is better informed." An equally impatient judge is reported to have said: "Mr. Smith, all that you are saying to me simply goes in at one ear and comes out at the other." "Yes, my lord," said Smith, "What is there to stop it?"

I was able, on another occasion, by the appropriate procedure, to get into the Strangers' Gallery at the House of Commons to listen to the proceedings. The House was in the middle of debating some extraordinarily dull subject, and I began to feel that the standard of debate was worse than that of a village debating society, when something quite dramatic and almost unprecedented happened, something which one might have had to wait years to see. Three somewhat truculent members from the region of the Clyde (Maxton, Buchanan and one other) seized the Mace and attempted to remove it. The Speaker hurriedly sent for Black Rod, and the three were gently but firmly escorted out of the Chamber by him. This was all very exciting.

And so, at the mature age of twenty-one, I found myself on the Medical Register as a duly qualified and legally qualified medical practitioner. It is popularly thought that, upon qualification, newly qualified doctors take an oath called the Hippocratic Oath (referred to occasionally by some cynics as the *hypocritic* oath). I can only say that I swore no such oath, although I may have sworn some others. The Hippocratic Oath is sworn only, I think, at a very limited number of medical schools or universities. Hippocrates was, of course, the famous Greek physician who lived in the fifth century B.C. and is sometimes referred to as the "Father of Medicine".

It was Bernard Shaw, while I was a student, who came to Bart's and addressed the students on "The Advantages of Being Unqualified". Early in his address – after several references to his old uncle who was a doctor in Ireland – he brought the house down by modestly saying that he, Shaw, of course did not know the difference between a tuberculous joint and a traumatic dislocation. He then went on to say that the advantages of being medically qualified were very few; they were, he said, merely that you could sue for your fees, and that you could sign death certificates. If unqualified, however, you could advertise to your heart's content, and you would make a great deal more money.

This position remains unchanged at the present time. Hence the quite lucrative practices of various practitioners, quite unqualified by law, who live on the various weaknesses of human nature; I am making no complaint of this, but merely pointing out that it is within the law to practise (and to charge for) all kinds of treatment and therapy, so long as the practitioner, whether he be naturopath, osteopath, manipulator or otherwise, does not "hold himself out" as the law puts it, or represent himself, as a legally qualified medical practitioner.

Soon after qualification I began to act as locum tenens in various parts of the country when doctors were away from their practices. These, usually of course fairly short engagements, were arranged through the registrar of the medical school at Bart's, who acted as a kind of agent in these matters. Some interesting, and at times curious things happened on these occasions.

On, I think, the first such occasion a young girl came into the consulting room, and on being asked the usual questions, she said that she had a lump in her neck which was causing her considerable concern. I examined her neck very carefully, and could find not the slightest trace of any lump. Thinking that this information would immediately alleviate her condition and her anxiety, I said very firmly: "There is no lump in your neck." At this, she rose from her chair, gave me a most indignant look, and stalked out of the room. I had failed, and no doubt had lost my principal and his practice a patient.

I realised that although my mind had been stuffed with details of diseases, many of them rare and obscure, I knew nothing about people and the way that their minds worked, nor had anybody bothered to teach me anything about this. No doubt a more experienced practitioner would have approached this case in a totally different manner. He certainly would not have said what I had said. He would have sympathetically made it clear that he recognised and understood precisely what the lady's trouble was (better still if he could say that he had recently and successfully treated precisely such a condition in another patient), and he would most certainly have prescribed some drug or treatment. It would, of course, have been immaterial what the drug or treatment was, because it must have been certain in due course that the patient's symptoms, being based on no organic condition, would disappear, and she would have gratefully credited the doctor with her cure.

An incident still remains in my memory of another locum tenens which I was doing in a country district. I had been called out to see a new case, a married woman at her house. Repeated knocks and rings at the front door eventually produced the figure of the lady in a night-dress at the window of an upper room. She threw the front door key down at my feet and invited me to enter. I did so, and comported myself, so far as I remember, very properly and with the utmost discretion. But I did hope later that there had been no witnesses of this occasion, or, if there were any, that they had not drawn a false conclusion from what they had seen. I also belatedly remembered the advice that we had been given at medical school – never to examine a female patient in the absence of a respectable and reliable chaperon. I am sure that I was not the only one occasionally to forget this advice in the exigencies and pressures of practice.

On another occasion, in a country practice, a man came in, but on seeing me he expressed his surprise, and I also sensed his lack of approval of what he saw. "Ain't Dr.— 'ere?" he asked. I explained the position as far as I could. "Dr.—" he went on, "you might say, he understands me better than what 'e understands 'isself." This seemed to put the position in a nutshell, but we got on quite well together after that.

Once I was asked by the registrar to go to a particular practice as locum, but was asked to comport myself suitably; on further enquiry, I was told that the circumstances were particularly sad since the principal of the practice had just died. I of course fully understood, and assumed an appropriately grave demeanour. I arrived at the doctor's house to find his widow listening to the latest collection of jazz records.

It was quite clear to me that the sort of case and situation that one met in general practice was very different from the classic and rare diseases upon which one's training had been based in a large London teaching hospital. On another locum tenens occasion I found myself unsuccessfully attempting to treat a sick child; the child had a persistently high temperature, the cause of which I had been quite unable to discover. The child's parents were rightly and naturally distressed and worried about this, and I thought it right, and they agreed, to call into consultation another doctor, a general practitioner. On the appointed day, this gentleman arrived at the child's house in a magnificent car, complete with uniformed chauffeur. In a bawdy manner, he pointed towards the chauffeur, saying, "What do you think? His name's Love, and he's never had a woman."

After we had seen the child together, we then saw the mother and father, and my consultant friend most impressively assured the parents that there was nothing to worry about, and that the child would get better. They were of course delighted, and clearly our consultant friend had made a deep and favourable impression. After we had left the house, I asked him what he thought was the matter with the child. "I have not the least idea", he said. But he was quite right in his ultimate view, and the child recovered completely.

These and other experiences confirmed the view that I had formed of the vast difference between the academic world of medicine in a teaching hospital and the world of general practice. It was most important, obviously, for the doctor to have a working knowledge of how people *thought*, and how their minds worked and reacted to disease, and the fear of disease. We had not been taught about these matters at medical school.

It was also important, I found, to be familiar with the kind of language and phraseology that ordinary people used. When a woman came in to see me and told me that she had not been to the House of Lords for a week, I found that my limited Parliamentary experience was of no use to me. Further tactful questioning revealed that she was referring to the state of her bowels. Whilst on this subject I am reminded of the patient who persisted whilst being examined by her doctor in repeating monotonously: "My heart belongs to Ireland. My heart belongs to Ireland." But the observant and alert doctor merely said to her: "Your heart may belong to Ireland, but your bowels are not in a free state."

Equally important was it for me to know what a woman meant when she informed me that she had not seen her courses lately. I learnt that I must dismiss from my mind all questions of racing horses or dogs; what I was being told was that the patient's menstrual cycle had been interrupted or delayed.

This must be the moment when I must ask the reader's indulgence to allow me to tell one more story, which has nothing to do with dogs, horses or women. It has to do with a small boy who was asked at school to write a short essay on Sir Francis Drake. His entry went something like this: "Sir Francis was on Plymouth Hoe, playing bowls, when a messenger came running up to him, saying: 'Sire, Sire, the Spanish Armada is here.' Sir Francis answered: 'The Spanish Armada can wait, but my bowels can't'."

Whilst doing another locum tenens, I found myself in a somewhat difficult and embarrassing situation. I was doing the work of a doctor who had gone away on his honeymoon, leaving me to share the house with his father, also a doctor. Father also happened to be the local coroner. One day I was giving an anaesthetic at the local hospital. I did not altogether like the methods and techniques of the operating surgeons, and I was not entirely surprised when the patient ceased to show signs of life. There then followed a curious procedure whereby the patient was hurried back to the ward, where resuscitative measures failed to produce any result, and death was formally certified. It was clear to me that nobody was proposing to inform the coroner about this death. But I had to have lunch with him, and I felt that at least the matter should be mentioned to him. Choosing, therefore, a convenient moment with the coffee after lunch, I told him about it. "Oh," he said, "That's all right. So long as she did not die on the table, I am not concerned." He was evidently not disposed to dissent from the local custom. I had at least done my duty, as I saw it, and had informed him. I may add that the precise part of the hospital in which death is certified is quite irrelevant in a case of this kind, but I believe that the perpetuation of this kind of legal fiction is not uncommon.

Another incident which occurred while I was acting as locum tenens is perhaps worth recording. Although a car had been provided for my use during the day, the arrangements for a night call in this part of Somerset seemed to be somewhat haphazard.

One evening, just as I was about to go to bed, there was a ring at the door, and a man asked if I could come out to an outlying village to see an aged woman relative of his. I said that I would do so, provided that they could get a car for me. Soon afterwards a car drew up. I got inside it, the man got into it, and then another man, whom I took to be another relative, took his seat in the car. Off we went through miles of dark, winding country roads. Nobody said a word, and eventually we drew up at a cottage, which was completely dark except for an upper room which showed a light. I was ushered up some ricketty stairs into this room, and there found an elderly woman who was having repeated convulsions or fits. So far as I was able to ascertain, she had not had any previous attacks of this kind, and after examining her I indicated that I took a very pessimistic and unhopeful view about her chances of recovery. I then went down the stairs and got back into the car. The two men got into the car. Then, just as we were about to move off, a third man got in and sat beside me. Back we went through the same dark country roads. All was silence, and then the third man leaned towards me and said, in a rich West-country burr: "Excuse me, zurr, but what doo 'ee really think to 'er?" I replied: "Why? Are you another relative of the old lady?" "No, zurr," he said, "Oi'm the undertaker."

Evidently news travels fast in Somerset. I am very happy to say that I was completely wrong, and that the old lady recovered in spite of any treatment she had received from me.

After qualification and the various experiences which I have already recounted, I thought it wise to try to get the experience which only resident or "house" hospital appointments could give. Rightly or wrongly, I assumed that it would be difficult to get these most coveted appointments at Bart's, so I did not apply there, and I got my experience as House Physician and House Surgeon at two provincial hospitals. I think that, apart from the unique atmosphere and skills which are associated with a London teaching hospital, the experience gained by those like myself was probably more valuable, since in many cases the honorary staff were very much occupied with their practices outside the hospital and one was therefore left to proceed with necessary treatment independently (subject, of course, to eventual change or correction by the consultant). I remember one somewhat eccentric physician, into one of whose beds I had admitted a patient, for whom I had written an appropriate prescription. The physician, who was, after his fashion, meticulous as well as eccentric, duly saw the patient later and then addressed me as follows: "Well, Baron, that is a very good prescription that you have written, but if I were you I would cross it out and write this one instead." He then proceeded to dictate a prescription of the precise drugs and quantities that I had ordered, except for a difference of one minim (one drop) in one of the more unimportant constituents. I held my peace, and did what he suggested.

Another physician consultant whose patients I looked after was an impressive character. He had been knighted, not because he was a distinguished doctor, which in my view he was not; he had become Sir— because of his work in local government – he had been major of the town, and practised as a general practitioner in it. He had a sententious and weighty manner, and twirled a monocle skilfully and with great effect.

I, like most hospital residents, worked fairly hard and at all hours. One day I found myself running a temperature, and as a well-behaved and dutiful houseman, I duly reported this to Sir—. "Ah, yes," he said: "You've got a touch of 'flu," and then ordered me to bed. After a few days in bed my temperature came down, and I resumed work. But, after some days on duty, the high temperature returned and I was clearly still unwell. Then an idea struck me. Among the patients I was looking after were some suffering from a mild infection of paratyphoid B; this is a kind of poor relation of typhoid fever proper, and much less serious than typhoid itself. Could I have acquired this infection? The only way of being sure of the diagnosis in cases of this kind is the taking of a blood test, and I asked one of my resident colleagues to withdraw the required amount of blood from my vein and send it to the pathological laboratory. Back came the report. I did in fact have paratyphoid B.

Now came the difficult moment. I had to report to Sir— that I had had the temerity and presumption to make my own diagnosis; he dealt with this state of affairs very promptly and firmly by putting me to bed on a diet limited to milk and water. This was the standard dietetic treatment for typhoid proper, where there is often ulceration of the intestine, and solid food might cause perforation of the bowels. By a curious coincidence, at about this time, I read an article in the *British Medical Journal* by a doctor of authority in these matters advocating a much more normal diet in typhoid cases, unless there was evidence of intestinal ulceration. There was no such evidence in my case and I was ravenous. Indeed I was rash, tactless, and intemperate, because I showed the article to Sir—. He was quite unimpressed by this, and stuck to his diet (or rather my diet). But the nursing staff were very sympathetic and kind, and I consumed, with their help, many items of food which Sir— would not have approved. None the less, two months or so of this combined treatment left me several stones lighter in weight. I eventually recovered in spite of treatment. Apropos of this, I am always reminded of the hospital which made the unhappy and unfortunately worded claim that within its walls nobody was allowed to die without medical assistance.

I and my fellow residents at the hospital relieved the monotony of hospital life on one occasion by mixing some of the luncheon cheese (which was notoriously bad) with some water, labelling it as pus taken from a fictitious patient, and sending it to the pathological laboratory. The report came back, saying: "Streptococci seen in large numbers. Would advise vaccine". Knowing the hospital cheese, we felt that this must be sound advice.

Later, I was appointed a medical officer at a large mental hospital a short distance outside London. The appointment offered a number of attractions, rather of the wrong sort. The countryside was delightful, tennis was available, work was light, food was good, and the salary at least acceptable. The nursing staff were also friendly and kind. I found the experience at this hospital of very great interest. Treatment of mental cases in those days was not as specialised as it now is – in fact there was no specific treatment for most of the cases. Of the acute admissions – those who suffered a severe mental breakdown for the first time – most cases would recover in any event (although of course they might suffer a second breakdown at some later time). In these present times of modern drug treatment, electro-convulsive treatment and, in the hands of some enthusiasts, actual brain surgery, I would doubt whether the overall recovery rate is very different from what it then was.

The medical superintendent, who had long ceased to be a doctor and had become very much more the administrator, seemed to have very little real or detailed knowledge of what went on in the hospital. He would proudly escort visitors round some of the wards, explaining that in the bad old days the ward would have been full of noisy, maniacal, and excited patients. Now, he said, thanks to good nursing, all was quiet. What he did not know was that, quite irregularly and by various stratagems, the patients had all been heavily sedated with drugs by the nursing staff.

I must confess that there were some wards in the hospital which I frankly feared to enter. These were the wards housing the chronically maniacal and violent patients. I, of course, had a key to the locked ward, and on entering, it was quite usual to find oneself surrounded by a menacing, uncontrollable, and violent group of patients whose attitude was clearly hostile. I am speaking now of the male wards; I used to attempt to look unconcerned, and hopefully look to see if a male nurse was coming to my assistance; usually he did, and I am glad to say, beyond occasionally having certain bedroom receptacles thrown at me (these were fortunately unbreakable), I escaped any serious injury. My experience of mental cases I found most useful later in general practice. I was usually able to recognise those breakdowns which were going to get better, and to give a comforting and reassuring prognosis to the relatives.

One was expected to take part in the social functions organised for the patients. Dances were not too difficult, but cricket matches presented some problems. One was liable to be struck quite hard with a ball aimed by one of the more excited patients, or even struck by one of them with a cricket bat.

Of modern psychiatry I have little knowledge, but I have always tended to treat any psychiatric opinion with reserve. In the United States and elsewhere, frequent sessions on the psychiatrist's couch may be followed by the psychiatrist almost dominating the patient's life and outlook. There is, in this connection, a medico-legal story which is worth repeating. A woman of some wealth was charged with shoplifting, an offence of which she was in fact undoubtedly guilty. She consulted her solicitor, who was a very experienced lawyer and a man of the world. He also knew that in cases of this kind a psychiatrist's opinion might very well be of assistance to the defence. He therefore sent his client to a psychiatrist, asking him whether there was anything from the psychiatrist's point of view which might assist the defence. In due course he received a letter from the psychiatrist which was on these lines:

Dear Mr.—

I have seen and examined your client Mrs.—. I am sorry that I am unable to suggest anything from my point of view which would assist her defence. I can only advise that in future she should take things more quietly.

Yours,etc.

I found life with the lunatics (as they were then plainly and tactlessly called) pleasant and undemanding. We now have mental hospitals, mental illness and mental patients only. Many of the chronic patients would never leave the hospital and would end their days there. In the case of many of these,

I made the discovery that many had made before me: that many of them were more sane and sensible than some people outside the hospital walls. But they knew when they were well off, and appreciated their free board and lodging. Some, indeed, were so institutionalised that it was doubtful if they could have survived economically in the outside world. Many, in any event, had no relatives who could have looked after them. But it was a curious and significant thing when the names of some of them appeared on a list of patients whose cases were to be reviewed on a question of possible discharge (and the patients would learn of this) there would be a strange recurrence of an earlier delusion, or symptoms of a renewed mental breakdown. One wondered. The occasional tedium of life at the hospital for the staff was also relieved by the receipt of extravagant and uninhibited love letters from some female patients.

I spent some eighteen months in this hospital. Although life for me was easy and not very exacting, I began to feel that unless I made the positive effort of leaving the hospital, I would become as institutionalised and fossilised as some of the patients – perhaps even as mad as they were. It would have been, of course, easier to stay where one was, but I was certain that I would have been wrong to have done so. I began to make enquiries about the possibilities of practice elsewhere, and eventually agreed to enter a partnership in general practice in London.

In those days (1928) the National Health Service as we now know it did not exist. There was, of course, Lloyd George's "panel". This was the list of employed persons entitled to free medical attention. The unemployed wives and children were required to pay for medical attention.

I enjoyed general practice, as far as it is possible to enjoy a way of life which leaves one at the beck and call of several thousand people at any time of the day or night. I always felt that medical practice would have been very much more a pleasant way of life if one were not forced all the time to consider the financial aspect of it – fees, when to charge and what to charge, and regrettably in some cases how to obtain payment at all of fees from someone who, although well able to pay them had no intention of doing so.

What has changed in my lifetime is the attitude of the public towards the medical profession. Fifty years ago the profession (including general practitioners) was highly respected – indeed in the case of some members of it even venerated. If one is to be frank, they were frequently credited with much more knowledge and skill than they really possessed. Now all that has gone, and the doctor – particularly the poor general practitioner – is treated with scant respect. He has become – and it is partly his own fault – a filler-up of forms and a prescriber of pills. Of course the poor man is hard pressed, and is trying to do the impossible for too many patients in too few hours, and the real fault lies in the administrative and political levels.

The present troubles of the National Health Service are well known and need no description from me. Doctors, in my view, have never been skilled negotiators, and, when dealing with astute and skilful politicians, tend to get the worst of the bargain. A skilled negotiator does not have to be a doctor, and I would have thought it perhaps desirable for the profession to seek such representatives outside their own ranks. Can one imagine the legal profession agreeing to the setting up of a National Legal Service akin to the National Health Service?

An unusual incident occurred in my practice. I had prescribed some medicine and liniment to a healthy young woman with some back trouble. A somewhat careless dispensing chemist transposed the labels on the bottles, so that the obedient patient did what the label indicated, and swallowed the liniment. My lunch was interrupted by an urgent call when the mistake was realised, and, by passing a stomach tube I was able to minimise the damage. I heard afterwards that my patient, an astute business woman, had been able to extract sufficient compensation from the chemist to enjoy a no doubt well deserved convalescence in Egypt.

A subject which has interested me for many years is that of abortion. It was following the Abortion Act of 1967 that those in the forefront of the advocacy of these matters made further attempts to secure the legalisation of euthanasia – something to which I shall refer later in this book.

One could not have been in medical practice for long, or

indeed could not have been in contemporary society for long, without realising that, whatever the law said, those women who were determined to obtain an abortion did obtain one. One knew that those with sufficient money were able to obtain an abortion in a nursing home with fees payable to certain doctors who had devised their own ways of circumventing the law. Those patients with little money went to what were known as the "back street" abortionists – whom one imagined as vaguely unpleasant people who, for a comparatively small reward, inexpertly and often incompletely procured an abortion with the limited and somewhat clumsy tools available to them.

The 1967 Act permitted Abortion on certain limited grounds, medical or social grounds in relation to the physical or mental health of the woman. It has turned out that the Act has virtually produced a situation in which abortion is available on demand – something which Parliament certainly never contemplated when it passed the Act.

As a coroner in later years I was not without experience of abortions. The sudden and mysterious collapse followed by death of a young woman immediately alerted one to the possibility of criminal abortion, and the fact of this would be demonstrated without difficulty by a pathologist if this in fact had occurred. Of course there was occasionally the case of a spontaneous abortion occurring, although this was much more rare than the induced variety. What happened very frequently at inquests on what were criminal abortions was that there was a conspiracy of silence, and nobody would say what one was sure they all knew – the identity of the abortionist.

Some doctors have deeply and conscientiously held views against inducing abortion, sometimes for religious reasons. They object to procuring abortion for mere "social" reasons; they would regard themselves as becoming mere technicians if they simply got rid of an unwanted pregnancy in this way. This has led to strikingly different degrees in the ease or difficulty that exists in getting an abortion done in different parts of the country. Once one is led to the consideration of "social" reasons for abortion, the doctor finds himself in the position, perhaps an unwelcome one, of acting as a judge. Some doctors have said, with some degree of disillusionment, that the abortion legislation has cast the doctors in the role of scapegoats in order to avoid society's responsibilities for the act of abortion; they say that the wide variations in its availability in the National Health Service are altered in the private sector; they say that in the private sector medical obstacles are replaced by financial ones.

An occasion occurred when I was in general practice in the early 1930's which is worth recording. I had agreed to act for a colleague during his absence on holiday. Among other appointments he held that of public vaccinator. It will be remembered that at that time vaccination, that is vaccination against smallpox, was compulsory by law for all children, except those whose parents had declared a conscientious objection to it before a magistrate before the child had reached the age of six months. The law has since been changed, as some think misguidedly. The procedure was that the doctor, the public vaccinator, was as a matter of routine sent a list of the names and addresses of all children who had reached the age of six months, and whose parents had not formally made any objection before a magistrate. It was the duty of the public vaccinator to "offer vaccination" to all such children. My own procedure was to send the parents a postcard saying that I would arrive for this purpose at their address at a certain time on a certain day.

I duly arrived at the house. This was a typically council estate kind of house. My knock at the door produced a small boy who opened it. The conversation then went something like this: "Is your mother in?" "No." "Is your father in?" "No." "Is the baby in?" "Yes." It was at this point, I am conscious with hindsight, that I went wrong. I told the boy that I was the public vaccinator. He clearly did not know what precisely this meant, and I explained to him that I was some kind of doctor. In any event, with his assistance (he holding the baby during the short operative period) I duly vaccinated the child, and continued my round of other visits.

When I returned home towards the end of the day, I learned that an angry and truculent father had presented himself at my front door, complaining of my conduct. I do not think that anybody could have produced any other result, or could have reasoned with him. Certainly my wife, who saw him, was not successful in pacifying him, and he departed from the house breathing fire and brimstone and announcing that he would "summons" me.

I am bound to say that I did not take this threat very seriously, but in a few days' time this unpleasant piece of paper did arrive. I must say that it looked rather horrifying. I was commanded to appear before the local magistrates to answer a charge that I "did assault one, so-and-so, to wit a female child" on the day in question. The matter was obviously one to which I had to give some thought.

Like most doctors in practice, I belonged, and had belonged for some years, to one of the medical defence societies – societies which defend one against allegations of professional negligence and similar proceedings. As I had paid my subscription to my society for many years without ever once requiring their assistance or services, it seemed to me that this was when they should act for me. I accordingly saw the secretary of my society (he was a retired medical officer of health) and told him my story. "Oh yes," he said, "You'll have to plead guilty." I replied that I did not propose to do this. "Yes," he said, "you'll have to plead guilty. I once took a swab from a child's throat for a diphtheria test without getting the parents' consent. I had to plead guilty. So will you."

I very firmly and politely said that I had no intention of doing anything of the sort, since all I had done was to do precisely what the law said had to be done. He saw that I was adamant, and then said: "Oh, well, would you like to see our solicitors?" I said that I would, and an appointment was made. "Our solicitors" proved to be a managing clerk, who at once said to me: "You'll have to plead guilty." I again made clear my complete rejection of this proposal, and after some further discussion he said to me: "Would you like us to send counsel to represent you?" I accepted this proposal. I am afraid that there is an obstinate streak in me which enables me, whilst listening to advice from many quarters, some of them said to be expert and professional, to make up my own mind finally as to which course I will take.

On the appointed day I duly presented myself at the magistrates' court. I was able to identify my counsel – a very young man who, I suspected, had not previously held a brief. We discussed the case. Counsel was armed with enormous volumes on the law of assault, and gave me graphic descriptions of various kinds of assault, none of which seemed to me to have much relevance to my own particular kind of alleged crime.

We tarried in the precincts of the court whilst various routine cases were dealt with – drunks, ladies of the town, and others. Eventually my case was called, and I was stood not inside, but just outside the dock. The complainant, the father, was placed in the witness box. The proceedings then went along these lines:

Clerk to Magistrates (to complainant): "You complain that this man (indicating me) assaulted your child?"
Complainant: "Yus."
Clerk: "What was the nature of the assault?"
Complainant: "Well, 'e come and vaccinate the baby be'ind me back." (This sounded a most acrobatic procedure.)
Clerk: "How is the child?"
Complainant: "All right."
Clerk: "Is the child any worse for the vaccination?"
Complainant: "No."
Clerk: "Have you any witnesses?"
Complainant: "Only the boy. 'E's at school."

There was then a rapid and whispered consultation between the magistrates and their clerk, followed by an announcement from the Chairman of the Bench: "Case dismissed".

My own view is that, at that stage, this was not a fair judicial decision, since, as it seems to me, a more fair and more proper decision would have been for the court to adjourn for the boy's evidence. He was, after all, a key witness, and the only witness for the prosecution.

But, had I taken the advice given to me, the result would have been quite different, and I would in fact have had a criminal conviction filed against my name. At least, I had avoided getting what my friends the police call a "record", or "form". I had avoided the conviction which I had been advised to accept.

An interesting situation arises, in my experience, when some lawyers are patients. I stress only SOME lawyers. The lawyer-patient tends to demand a clear "yes" or "no" to a medical question to a medical problem (in relation to his own illness) to which there can be no clear answer. Medicine, regrettably, is still an inexact science. The lawyer's approach to these questions is in contrast to many opinions of counsel which I have seen, in which counsel is very careful to hedge his bets on the lines of: "If it were to be shown that so-and-so is the case, it might well be held that . . . but if on the other hand so-and-so (the reverse) existed, a contrary decision might be reached". In the same way that I do not accept all medical opinion unreservedly, I am inclined to look with equal care and scepticism on legal advice. It often happens that two different parties embark with great confidence and at great expense into a civil battle against each other in the High Court. I have no doubt that both parties must have been advised that each had a reasonable chance of winning the case; one party is likely to find that it has had the wrong advice.

There is a curious difference in one's relations with one's patients or clients, depending upon whether the practice is one of medicine or that of law. A doctor is expected to give an instant opinion and advice on any health problem which is presented to him. A lawyer, and I think very properly so, makes no bones about it; he reaches out to his extensive bookshelves, selects a massive volume on the subject under discussion, and quite openly looks up the point of law in question, indeed unashamedly quoting to the client extracts from it. I may add that in my early days in medical practice I had concealed behind a screen a suitably small medical library. If I wanted some better advice, I would make an appropriate excuse to disappear behind the screen.

Perhaps, whilst on the subject of professional men as patients, something should be said of doctors as patients. Doctors are usually believed to be notoriously difficult and demanding patients – perhaps they are. I think that this position sometimes arises because the attending physician or surgeon assumes that the doctor-patient knows and understands all the problems associated with his illness; unhappily (sometimes happily) this is not always so, and the poor chap is quite ignorant of some of the interesting technicalities with which the great man is only too familiar. It ought to be remembered that when a doctor becomes ill he ceases to be a doctor, but is a patient, and like all patients with the apprehensions, fears, and doubts of all other patients, and should be treated as such. In addition, he has the very dubious disadvantage of knowing the risks to which he may be subject.

During my professional lifetime, of course enormous technological advances have been made in the practice and skills of medicine, pharmacology, anaesthesia, medical electronics and surgery. But at the base of this vast technical pyramid there is still a human being, the patient, and this vitally important fact is, I am sure, sometimes forgotten.

In dentistry, too, great advances have been made. I am old enough to remember the time when most dentists in Great Britain were unqualified, untrained, and simply ignorant. The Dentists Act of 1921 put them on the Dental Register for the first time, without any examination or qualification of any kind. I still have vivid and painful recollections of having suffered at their hands as a child. As "quacks" before the passing of the Dentists Act they were permitted to advertise. I remember one who used to advertise in the local newspaper with the striking slogan: "Teeth extracted with the greatest pains". I often think that one of the many things of our own era for which we should be grateful is modern and skilful, and usually painless, dentistry.

In 1930 there arose an opportunity for me which I thought I should accept. I was offered the post of ship's surgeon for a return trip from London to South America, lasting in all for two months. I felt that this was something that I ought not to miss, and my partners readily agreed to look after my patients in my absence. The ship was the *Highland Monarch* of the Nelson Line (now I think no longer in existence). It carried meat, passengers, and emigrants from Spain and Portugal to Brazil and the Argentine. The ports of call were to be Boulogne, Vigo, Lisbon, Rio de Janeiro, Montevideo and Buenos Aires. As well as myself, the ship carried a Spanish doctor and a Portuguese doctor. These two were responsible for the emigrants, who, being from a poorer background, were more likely to present medical problems. The less fortunate crew and other passengers had to rely upon me.

At the ports in Spain and Portugal I was supposed to stand at the top of the gangway, take an impossibly fleeting look at the emigrants, and to reject any medically unfit. Of course it would have been quite impossible to have done this by such a cursory look at them. After a few ports of call, I got rather tired of this proceeding, and preferred to go on tour of the port with one or two congenial passengers, leaving the inspection of the boarding emigrants to the practised eye of the sick-bay steward. He would keep on one side, for me to see, any of whom he had any doubts. This got me into some trouble with the Captain, when it turned out that we had let on board an epileptic. "This isn't a hotel, doctor", he remonstrated with me. I had to point out to him that the whole of Harley Street could not have diagnosed this on sight.

I well recall being fitted out with an elegant and suitably nautical uniform with braid, brass buttons, and all that went with it. Soon after we left the docks in London, I was walking up and down the deck with a considerable sense of satisfaction and self-importance when a lady passenger came up to me and demanded to know at what time tea was being served. I thought that this was an inappropriate enquiry to me; I drew myself up to my full height, and replied that this was not my department; the lady and I then parted company.

Fortunately I had very little medical work to do. Most of this was provided by the emigrants, for whom the Spanish and Portuguese doctors were responsible. Frequently during the still and dark hours of the night I would hear from the cabin of the Spanish doctor which was next to mine a quite audible conversation. It was between one of the sick-bay stewards and the doctor. It always ended in the same way: the doctor simply said: "*Manana*". It was borne upon me that what one had heard about this old Spanish custom was really true.

The whole trip was, for me, a delightful holiday experience. A thoughtful shipping company, however, had provided me with a comprehensive supply of drugs and surgical appliances, including a whole range of dental forceps, of which the precise method of use was unknown to me.

Early during the voyage, one of the crew presented himself to me with a dental condition; this was simply a very loose front tooth which he wished to get rid of. I suspect that almost any reader of this book could have removed this tooth without difficulty; indeed, I think that he could have done it himself. However, with proper professional gravity, I applied a pair of forceps, and out it came very easily. The seaman was delighted with me and must have gone back to the crew's quarters and given me a high recommendation to his colleagues. Next morning there was a queue outside my cabin-surgery waiting to see me. Heading the queue was a sailor with a very swollen face and obviously suffering from a dental abscess – a very different situation from that of my patient of the day before. But he was determined to get treatment from me. "I hear that you are very good with teeth", he said. There was no choice for me. I injected, very unskilfully, some cocaine around the tooth, and then embarked upon the operation. I pulled, and he leapt up into the air in agony, emitting blood-curdling shrieks of pain, and rushed out of the cabin. I looked outside my door. The queue had vanished, as if by magic.

I was struck by a fundamental difference between practice on a ship and practice on land. If one sees a patient on land, one prescribes something for him, and (since most conditions tend to get better in any event and are self-limiting) when he comes to see you in a week's time he will probably be better. But I found it somewhat embarrassing on board ship to see a patient and prescribe for him, and then, perhaps an hour later, on a walk on deck to run into him again. One would, of course, politely enquire how the patient was, only to receive the inevitable reply: "I'm no better, doctor."

On one occasion, I thought that I might have some serious work to do. The cry went up: "Man overboard". A crew member had fallen from some rigging. The ship slowed and turned around to look for him. Alas, no trace of him was found.

I learned that it was the practice that if the shipping line took out to Brazil or the Argentine an emigrant whom the Argentine or Brazil refused to accept on medical grounds it then became the duty of the shipping line to repatriate the emigrant. Accordingly, on the return trip, we took aboard at Buenos Aires a Frenchman who was said to be suffering from trachoma. This is a highly contagious and unpleasant eye condition. He was accordingly treated with distant respect and was kept isolated in what was normally used as the ship's equivalent of a padded cell; an isolated cabin in which he was kept with all the precautions one could take; all utensils and everything ever in contact with him disinfected and not used by anyone else; I must confess that I somewhat limited the number of my own visits to him. When the time came for him to disembark, we dropped anchor just outside Boulogne, and awaited the visit of the port medical officer. He proved to be a most impressive and enormous man, with an equally impressive and enormous beard. I told him the history, so far as I knew it, of this particular patient, and he penetrated into the padded cabin. After quite some time, he came out, looking singularly unruffled and undisturbed. I asked him: "*c'est un trachoma?*" "*Non, non*" he said, "*c'est un conjunctivitis.*" (This is a much more common and relatively innocuous condition.) If he were right, all our precautions had been unnecessary. But he took the patient back to Boulogne with him, and so one never knew the ultimate truth or outcome.

A passenger on board on the outward trip with whom and others I spent many a pleasant hour in the ship's swimming pool was Fred Majdalany, who was later, during the war, to play a part in the Allied attack on Monte Cassino, and to write a most successful book about this. Unhappily he has since died.

And so back to the docks in London. There had ended for me what had been a very pleasant and memorable holiday.

Other features of the voyage remain curiously in my mind – the daily inspection of the ship by the captain, accompanied by the chief engineer and me, when inevitably the "Old Man", as he was known, would step up to some meat hanging in the cook's quarters, with the inevitable and never-changing comment: "Fine piece of beef, doctor," to which I would mumble some unintelligible reply; the beauty of Rio and the Copocabana beach, together with my feeling that Rio exhibited in man every conceivable shade of skin from absolute white to absolute black; spending a fortnight on board in port up the River Plate, when my face attracted the attention of a large number of mosquitoes who bit me savagely.

Whilst on the sea and ships, I must revert to what we now somewhat sadly call "the good old days". My wife and I took a cruise shortly before the war. For the magnificent sum of thirteen pounds, we cruised for thirteen days from Liverpool, calling at ports in Spain and Morocco. This was truly magnificent value. It is quite true that for many passengers it was more of a "booze" than a cruise. One gentleman, after a very convivial evening, fell down a companionway and sustained fatal injuries. Thereafter his body was kept in refrigeration, and conveyed back to Liverpool on board. Of course we, as passengers, were tactfully kept unaware of this sad story, and only heard about it afterwards through somewhat unofficial sources.

Another case when I was in practice was that of a wealthy woman to whom I was called one morning by an anxious husband who had been quite unable to arouse her from sleep. She was in fact deeply comatose when I saw her. Beside her was an empty bottle with the label on it indicating that it had contained barbiturate sleeping tablets. The case was only too clear, and I knew that the likelihood of her surviving was very remote. In spite of this, and in everybody's interests (including my own, lest the family should feel that not enough had been done for the patient) I called out in consultation a distinguished physician, who performed, or attempted, various impressive and heroic attempts at resuscitation. None of these was of any avail, and after an hour or so it was clear that the patient was dead. My consultant colleague then said to me: "Let's go into the bathroom and wash our hands." We duly went into the bathroom and we washed our hands. Whilst drying his own, he looked around at the expensive furnishings of the house and then he said: "What was her trouble, do you think? Too much money?" I cannot recall what I answered, but it was not until several days later that I realised that what he had been doing was trying to assess the magnitude of the fee which he could charge. But that was all a long time ago. I must have been the first – or perhaps the only – prospective bridgegroom to take his future wife and future mother-in-law into the Divorce Court to listen to the proceedings so that they might understand and appreciate in what ways a marriage could go wrong. In fact they were nearly ejected from the court because of their frequent whisperings and laughter. The court was presided over by the President of the then Divorce, Probate and Admiralty Division, Lord Merrivale, who could sometimes be severe in his manner. One case which we heard was one in which the petitioner in evidence said that his wife had thrown a frying pan at him. "But", he added, "it didn't 'it me."

Divorce law and practice has changed since those days, but those were very múch the era of the machine-like processing of a chain of the so-called "hotel divorces", in which evidence was given on behalf of the petitioner, usually by a chambermaid or a porter, that the respondent was seen to be occupying a double bedroom with a person of the opposite sex, and who was not the petitioner. (The petition was undefended.) This evidence usually related to an occasion when the chambermaid or porter entered the room to serve morning tea. In one case the evidence proceeded along these traditional, almost hallowed, lines, but without any reference to the tea. This was too much for the learned judge, who almost seemed to think that this was a break with all precedent, because he intoned: "What? What? No cup of tea?" Nevertheless he gave the petitioner a decree nisi of divorce. By coincidence, we happened to see at the back of the court a well-known authoress (whose own divorce petition, as we later learned, was to come on later). She too was clearly learning the procedure of the court.

In 1933 I had married my dear wife, Kathleen, who has since gallantly tolerated my weaknesses and my peculiarities. We spent the first part of our honeymoon at Madeira, staying at one of the lesser hotels. On the island we met another honeymoon couple who were staying at the well-known Reid's Hotel. (They were later to become patients of mine and I was to deliver their firstborn.) They suggested that we should move to their hotel, but we pointed out the greater cost to us of such a move. However, enquiries were made and, surprisingly, the cost at Reid's was given as slightly less than we were already paying. We therefore moved in to Reid's, but our bill there, when it came, seemed to be inordinately large. I mentioned the quotation we had been given, but the hotel pointed out that this was a quotation for one person. There had been a most unfortunate misunderstanding, and our bill was at twice the rate we had understood. Fortunately I was just able, with difficulty, to pay it.

I have already referred to some aspects of foreign travel. On the pre-war cruise from Liverpool which I have mentioned, we were fascinated by the markets and souks of Morocco. At this time colour transparencies were being developed but were in their infancy, and I was able to get some interesting shots of our visit, showing the picturesque markets and piles of colourful melons and exotic fruits; I was reminded of the ancient Oriental aphorism: women for breeding, boys for pleasure, and melons for delight.

I have always enjoyed foreign travel. Language difficulties sometimes present problems. I have always delighted in being in France, because it is almost the only country whose language I can claim to speak. I remember, as we all do, the enviable days when five British pounds were represented by a beautifully white and very crinkly five pound note. On one occasion, being rather short of French currency, I decided to attempt to change one of these notes in the bank of the smallish town through which we were passing. This involved filling up all sorts of details on a form (possibly including the name of one's maternal grandmother). I did my best with whatever officialdom required at the counter. The cashier looked at my beautiful five pound note, then at me, then at the form. *Quel nom?* he said. *Ah! Baron*, he went on, *mais Baron Qui?* We got over this little local difficulty, and I got my currency.

A later holiday in Yugoslavia was less amusing, and certainly enabled me to study local life in a way that I had not anticipated. I became a patient. We were staying in a part of the country that I believe was formerly part of the old Montenegro. I became seriously ill, and found myself in the motor car of the local doctor on my way to hospital at Stari Bar. The doctor was accompanied by a young man who might be described as the sorcerer's apprentice (what the Germans call a *feldscher*). Luckily for my pocket the National Health Service in England has reciprocal arrangements with Yugoslavia. I was taken to a hospital high in the mountains – a very primitive building. There I was placed in a ward with five other male patients, and, with great kindness, my wife was provided with a bed beside me. This was most thoughtful of the hospital authorities, but a little embarrassing for her, since she had to dress and undress in the full gaze of the other patients; these gentlemen, I may say, made no concessions, and the manoeuvres and gyrations to which my wife was put were reminiscent of Brighton beach when ladies try to get in and out of bathing costumes without offending public decency. But, in all seriousness, this was a terrifying experience for my wife. She wanted, for example, a sleeping pill on the night of my admission. She tried her few words of German, but with no result. It ultimately turned out that the simple word "tablet" would have sufficed. None the less, I found the native population pleasant and friendly, sturdy and kind. Racially they were very mixed. There were obviously elements of Turk, Serbo-Croat and others. On one visiting day, my wife having for a short time gone to the nearby village, every other bed was surrounded by solicitous relatives, all of whom and brought presents of some kind for their sick relatives. I notice one such visitor clutching a parcel, and studying me with some interest.

I had gathered from earlier conversation and gestures that it had been explained to her that I was some kind of foreigner. Suddenly she came over to my bed and pressed the parcel into my hands. I tried to indicate to her that her own relative was the proper recipient of her gift, but to no avail. She was kindness personified.

The hospital facilities were very primitive, and the treatment virtually non-existent. One of my fellow patients had a persistent cough, which was not improved by the large number of cigarettes which he smoked. He also had the undesirable habit of walking about the ward during the night. I found that this did not assist my sleep.

I did not speak the local language at all. I found that when communications broke down otherwise, it was frequently the German language which was used; of this I only knew a few words. I did know that Yugoslavia was a communist or near-communist country. I was therefore not altogether surprised when a man appeared at the foot of my bed, dressed in a smart suit and wearing a very red tie and a very red pocket handkerchief. He was clearly not a doctor, but was obviously some kind of official. He stood at the end of my bed and looked through my charts and records. *Ah! Baron,* he said, *das ist ein aristokratischer name.* Something in my subconscious mind began to remind me of tumbrils and guillotines, and I hastily said "No, no. Me no aristocrat". I was glad to see him move away from my bed.

The hospital was in a remote part of the country. My wife found herself commuting to a hotel during the day to get a bath and a change of clothes. She also managed to get written out in Serbo-Croat the equivalent of "My husband is a patient in the hospital" in order to regain admission to the hospital.

She plucked up courage to wander to the near village on market days, and ran into some of our original English fellow travellers. She also passed some time in sketching the local countryside. She told me that two twelve or thirteen-year old boys talked to her, and were interested because she was English, and spoke a few English words. While all this was going on a dark-skinned boy went by. They threw a stone and spat at him. My wife reproved them; they replied that he was Turkish. She felt that she was again back with racial problems.

An official of the Yugoslav tourist agency came to see me in hospital. He was most kind and sympathetically helpful. My perverted sense of humour lead me to tell him that I had no intention of letting my illness spoil my holiday. Since the prospect quite clearly was that I might be spending several months in bed, that was a supreme understatement.

Every morning *Sestra* (Sister) would give me an intravenous injection. I do not think that this produced any appreciable improvement in my condition, but, as I was merely the patient, I duly submitted to it. On one of these occasions I noticed a bubble of air in the syringe – this I knew if injected into the blood stream would be fatal. I therefore deemed it right and proper by appropriate sign language to indicate to *Sestra* the existence of the air bubble. She seemed to understand what I was trying to say; indeed, it is likely that she was already aware of the situation and had no intention of pushing the piston of the syringe firmly home. None the less I was glad to have established this important piece of communication with her, and I duly survived.

After some time at this hospital, it was decided to move me to another hospital in Dubrovnik. I welcomed this, if for no other reason than that it brought me nearer to the airport from which planes took off to England. In due course of time the day arrived for my journey to Dubrovnik. All patients, male and female, at the hospital were dressed in the same colour of green pyjamas or nightdresses, and as the ambulance with me in it drove away, there were waves of good wishes to me from the green figures on the balconies and at the windows; it was like a film set from one of the more avant-garde film producers.

The Dubrovnik hospital was much bigger, but only marginally better in its available facilities. What we know as bed screens or curtains around individual beds appeared to be unknown in Yugoslavia, and I found myself the unwilling witness of some rather macabre scenes. I was, however, impressed with the skill and kindness of the many male nurses, whose attentions were a new experience, at least to me.

Each day the doctor in whose charge I was made his rounds. He was an enormous man. We had a common language in French. Each day he would stop at my bedside and ask: *Comment ça va?* Although I was far from well, I would usually diplomatically reply: *Mieux, merci*, or *Comme çi, comme ça.* On one occasion I felt that the only appropriate reply was a very Gallic gesture in which I extended my arms widely and shrugged my shoulders, meaning "What on earth do you expect me to say?" I think that he knew what I meant, because he hurriedly moved to the next bed.

Eventually the time arrived for me to take off on my flight from Dubrovnik airport. My son-in-law, John, very kindly flew out to collect me. Although my tickets were carefully marked "Stretcher case", nobody seemed to take much notice of this, and I was required to go up the gangways and stairs just like anybody else.

We arrived at Heathrow Airport where an ambulance was waiting for me on the tarmac, in charge of a charming and efficient airport sister. I was touched to find myself also greeted by my coroner's officer who covered London Airport, Police Constable Jack Little (the airport was, after all, within my jurisdiction as coroner – this was now in 1967 – and was one which usually provided a fertile source of work for me). How wonderful it was to hear and speak English, and to know that I was in good hands. I was whisked off to one of London's teaching hospitals and eventually restored to health. I had seen little of Yugoslavia except that limited view which one gets through a hospital window, and my final feeling was that despite the kindness and medical facilities available it was on the whole undesirable to be seriously ill in a country whose language one could not speak at all. It is at least desirable to be able to make known the state of one's bowels to the staff!

An interesting sequel followed all this. I had taken out, through the official tourist agency, an insurance policy which, I understood, covered this kind of emergency. When, on returning to England, I made my claim, the insurance company replied that they were not liable, because, under the terms of the policy, any claim had to be made within fourteen days of the "incident" occurring, and I had not done this. (I could not have done it, both because of my illness and because all the necessary papers were in England.)

This attempted repudiation by the insurance company of its clear moral duty (if not its strict legal one) made me somewhat angry, and I wrote to them that if they proposed to deal with my claim in this way, I would suggest to the travel agency that they placed the insurances of their clients elsewhere. I received a reply from the insurance company that in view of what I had written they would "naturally" meet my claim. I very much liked the use of the word "naturally".

I have always had some difficulty in remembering at the proper time to get my passport renewed. On one occasion my wife and I flew to Amsterdam. The British passport official saw nothing wrong, but on arrival in Holland the Dutch looked sternly at our out-of-date passports. I made apologetic noises, but they said that I must put the matter right by calling at the British Embassy. We were in fact staying at The Hague, and by coincidence the next morning Queen Wilhelmina was opening the Dutch Parliament. The streets were crowded with serried ranks of spectators on the pavements. I approached a Dutch policeman to enquire the whereabouts of the British Embassy. These magic words produced the most dramatic result. He saluted us smartly, and divided the crowds to let us through, and directed us to the Embassy. But when we got to the Embassy, no one was there except for a very tired and very bored clerk, who said that we must go to the Embassy in Rotterdam. At this stage, I decided to do nothing. It seemed to me that if they had let us come in to the country, as they had, they were certain to let us out. And so it proved; events went into reverse: the Dutch noticed the imperfections of our passports, the British not at all.

On another occasion, whilst on holiday in Rome, I again became a patient. My daughter Valerie, now a very attractive young woman, used to love going off by herself to view the sites and ancient monuments of Rome, perhaps a not altogether wise procedure. She had in fact a good command of the Italian language. It was not at all unusual for her to lose her way, and we were never surprised to see her being escorted back to the hotel by two gallant and helpful Roman policemen. She attracted the attention of a young Italian man who proposed to take her to visit the Tivoli gardens and fountains some miles outside Rome. He had a small Fiat car and perhaps unnecessarily (but no doubt out of respect for our grey hairs) invited us to accompany them. We did this, and our young Italian driver never seemed to be doing less than seventy miles an hour. The car had a sunshine roof, which was open. In retrospect, I think that this was a factor in what later happened.

Our young friend returned with us in the car to our hotel. The moment I alighted from the car, my nose began to bleed copiously, something that I had not suffered previously. I did not regard this as being in any way serious, but I found that for the next few days life was somewhat difficult. I would be in the middle of an excellent meal at the hotel, when I would have to retire hurriedly to my room because of the bleeding. Finally, as one does in this sort of situation, I consulted the hotel porter with a view to getting medical aid. He strongly recommended a doctor somewhere high up in the hills who, he averred, had done wonders for his mother-in-law (whether by keeping her alive or otherwise I was not quite sure). I did not somehow feel that this was the man for me. He then said that he would ask a local doctor to come and see me, and this was arranged by telephone for the next day. I then discovered that doctors in Rome are very much like doctors elsewhere; this one did not come to see me. The mountain therefore went to Mahomet, and I called on the doctor in his rooms in the fashionable Via Veneto. There were obviously expensive furnishings, carpets, and pictures there, and when I entered the consulting room with my bleeding nose the doctor indicated, with mildly deprecatory gestures, that he would prefer his carpet not to become bloodstained. I immediately produced my handkerchief.

I had in my mind that this bleeding could be treated by some form of electric cautery. The doctor agreed that this was so, but said that since it was Holy Week, most consultants were on holiday. However, he made a telephone call to someone who was *Il Professore*. There was a reference to me: *Nostro Collegio Inglese*, and the professor agreed to see me at a nursing home on the Janiculum hill. I was taken there by taxi. The great man inserted what looked like a screwdriver into my nose, manipulated it, and all was well. The white-robed Sister was good enough to say that I was very brave. This was merely a professional exaggeration. But although I could happily have done without this incident, I felt that it had given me an insight into a side of Roman life which I would not otherwise have seen.

On another occasion, in Majorca, I had some unpleasant eye symptoms, about which I did not bother to seek advice for some time. An appointment was made for me to see, after more delay by me, a doctor in Palma. I carefully consulted my Spanish dictionary, and prepared a suitable speech in Spanish to describe my symptoms. Proceeding to Palma on a very hot day, we found the waiting room full of Majorcans, many of whom had obviously been waiting for a very long time. After a long wait of two hours or so, I entered the consulting room. Now I was seized with stage fright. My carefully prepared Spanish phrases completely eluded me. I broke into French, which fortunately he seemed to understand. He examined me, and then delivered his verdict in a loud stentorian voice. At first I could not understand what he was saying. *C'est une manifestation allergique*, he said. *Une manifestation quoi?*, I rejoined. *Allergique*, he bellowed, *On va vous guérir*. This was at least comforting. He wrote out a prescription, his receptionist extracted a fee from me, and I departed. I went to some trouble at the pharmacy to explain that I was, so to speak, in the trade. I think, on reflection, that this merely put up the price that I was called upon to pay. However, in a week or so I had recovered. But I must now return to earlier years.

By 1936 I had been in general medical practice for eight years – leaving out the years of my earlier resident hospital jobs – and I was in serious doubt as to whether I wished to continue with it. It was physically a strenuous life, and one's patients were not always necessarily grateful for what one was able to do for them. I knew, of course, that practice at the Bar was precarious and that such a practice was not easily acquired. I did, however, have some not unfriendly solicitor contacts and, after a particularly sleepless night, my mind was made up and I made the decision to get called to the Bar, as I was entitled to, having completed the required examinations in 1926, on the next Call Night at the Middle Temple. One's application to be called had to be supported by a Bencher of the Inn, and I was fortunate enough to be able to get this from the then Director of Public Prosecutions, Sir Edward Tindal Atkinson. My long-suffering wife, who probably privately thought that I had lost my reason, agreed with what I proposed to do. We were, I pointed out, not really giving any hostages to fortune, since we had no children. This deficiency was of course duly remedied later by the physiological processes of nature resulting in the welcome and happy birth of our daughter, Valerie, about two years later.

And so on Call Night in 1936, with other aspiring tyros all duly robed and bewigged, I was duly called to – in that delightful phrase – "the utter bar" (that is, the outer or junior bar) by Serjeant Sullivan, K.C., one of the last of the Irish Serjeants practising in England. This was a memorable night. The beautiful Middle Temple Hall was later to be bombed to pieces during the war, then later still to be miraculously restored to its former majesty by building and architectural experts.

I entered the chambers of Gerald Slade. He was later to become Mr. Justice Slade, but also, unfortunately, to die at a relatively early age. He had a very busy common law practice, with a good deal of libel and slander, on which he was an acknowledged authority.

I found life at the Bar a very pleasant one – subject always to the grim necessity of finding enough work upon which to subsist. I was, however, fortunate in being able to get hold of some of those much desired briefs. I would not say, however, that these early cases were legal contests of the greatest moment, important though they were to me. I remember one in which I had a kind of double professional interest.

A married woman had become pregnant and had attended her general practitioner during the pregnancy. He had assured her (as was no doubt the case) that everything was normal and that all would go well. When the time for her delivery came, things did not go so well at first. It was obvious to her general practitioner that consultant help was required. Unfortunately the husband of the patient was at that time many hundreds of miles away on business, and it was not possible to contact him. The doctor therefore took it upon himself to call out an obstetrician, who, together with an anaesthetist, very skilfully and efficiently delivered a most acceptable and living child, in what had then turned out to be a "breech" presentation. (This means that instead of, as normally, the head presenting first, in this case the buttocks of the infant first appeared; hence the difficulties that had arisen.) Perhaps none of this was so very exceptional or unusual. What was unusual, according to the instructions I received from the solicitors, was the attitude of the husband upon receiving a very modest account from the obstetrician. The husband took the point that he had never authorised the consultant being called in, and that he was not liable, and he refused to pay the account.

I was instructed to appear at Bloomsbury County Court before Judge Sir Alfred Hill-Kelly on behalf of the consultant, who took the not surprising view that he ought to be paid for the work that he had done. All this was, of course, before the birth of the National Health Service.

The facts, although simple, involved a point of law which is called "agency of necessity". This means that in certain circumstances, and I was instructed to press that the facts in this case came within those circumstances, one man – in this case the general practitioner – can properly and rightly incur a liability for another, in this case the husband.

His Honour Sir Alfred Hill-Kelly had something of a reputation among the junior Bar as a difficult judge before whom to appear, and it was with some trepidation that I went to Bloomsbury County Court armed with my robes and with a number of heavy books covering the law of agency of necessity. After sitting through some other cases, my case was called. I thereupon got up and opened the case with a graphic description of the facts to His Honour, including a somewhat technical account of what a "breech" case was and what it entailed. I detected some signs of impatience on the Judge's face, and he eventually interrupted me with: "*You* give the evidence very well; I should like to hear the witnesses." "If your Honour pleases," I replied, and called the obstetrician, who gave evidence along the lines of the facts that I have outlined. At this point His Honour called out: "Where's the Husband?" A small and rather reluctant-looking man at the back of the court nervously came forward, whereupon the Judge said to him: "Why don't you pay him? He saved your wife's life and produced a healthy child." There was no very distinct reply from the husband, whereupon the Judge said: "Judgement for the Plaintiff," and my case was won. This was clearly rough justice, I thought, but very just justice, and I did not have to argue the abstruse legal points which I had anticipated.

One of the first briefs I received from a well-wishing solicitor was to appear in the Companies Court (then presided over by Mr. Justice Crossman – father of the late Richard Crossman). My instructions were to ask on behalf of a creditor for a winding-up order for a company, then in obvious financial difficulties. I was told that the proceedings would be purely formal, and that all I had to do was to ask for "the usual order", and that my application would be unopposed. That morning in court, as I awaited my case to be called, my knees, in the Biblical phrase, "smote one against the other". Eventually the case was called. I got up and nervously said my piece, whereupon his Lordship said, no doubt correctly, that he could not hear me.

I then said it a little louder, and I added, for good measure, that I understood that there was no opposition to the order for which I was asking. At this moment at least half a dozen gentlemen all wearing wigs, who said that they represented other creditors or other interests, all rose and said that they most emphatically DID oppose a winding-up order. At this stage, conscious that my coat was being pulled by an anxious solicitor's clerk, and not having the least idea what to do, I was relieved to hear his Lordship say that he would adjourn the proceedings for a week. At the next week's hearing all was harmony, the parties in the meantime having composed their differences.

Whilst in chambers in the Temple, I used to leave my car in a street just off the Thames Embankment. One day I received a document requiring my presence at Bow Street Court, on the alleged grounds that I had caused what the law calls "unnecessary obstruction" with my car. Ignoring the old and wise adage that he who represents himself has a fool for a client, I did precisely that before the then Chief Magistrate, Sir Rollo Graham-Campbell. The only prosecution witness was a large policeman, who proved a not very difficult target, even for my immature advocacy. I had done my homework, and he had not. I had, for example, measured the width of the road, which he wildly and wrongly estimated. At any rate, after a while the case against me was dismissed. I asked for costs against the police, but this was too much for the magistrate, and he refused.

Thereafter my strategy went wrong. I continued to leave my car in the same place, and a second summons for Bow Street arrived for me. Flushed with my former success, I again represented myself before a different magistrate. With almost indecent insolence, I told him that the Chief Magistrate had already decided that leaving a car in this exact position did not constitute obstruction. With ill-controlled irritability, he told me that he did not want to know what another magistrate had said on a different occasion. And, to make things worse, this time there were two police officers, and not just one of them; they both said firmly that my car was causing an obstruction. Result: fine of forty shillings.

After one year in chambers at the Bar, and the prospect of the Long Vacation, the thought of a holiday seemed very attractive. Obviously, in the circumstances, one costing less money would be more attractive. An advertisement in the *British Medical Journal* caught my eye. "Hospitality locum", it said, was offered on the Devon coast; further and better, as the lawyers say, it added that work was nominal. This seemed to offer what was required, and I got in touch with the advertiser and agreement was reached.

In due course my wife and I arrived at the doctor's house, and he and his family departed for their own holiday. What, unfortunately, the doctor had omitted to tell me was that he had undertaken to attend the confinements of a large number of ladies who were likely to go into labour at about the time I was there. This they promptly proceeded to do, usually between the hours of two and four in the morning. I was not precisely delighted with this uncovenanted re-entry into the world of obstetrics. I remember one particular case in the early morning darkness to which I had been called, and in which I had considerable difficulty in finding the patient's house. I at last found a policeman on night duty, and asked for his help, which he readily gave. I must have told him what it was all about, and must have expressed my dissatisfaction with ladies who timed things so inconveniently that I had had to leave my warm bed. He, very clearly and very much a family man and a man of a logical turn of mind, suggested that since all these new arrivals had probably been begotten at night it was only to be expected that they would arrive at about that time. I must confess that I had not considered the matter from this point of view, but, since he was a person in authority, I though it tactful to agree with him.

Some years at the Bar, later, had produced a restlessness in me, and a feeling that my own particular qualifications ought to be more specifically and more usefully channelled. I called upon Mr. Ingleby Oddie, the coroner for Central London, whose activities and observations very frequently figured on the pages of the London evening papers. He was kind enough to let me sit with him both in his court and in his office, and I was able to obtain a working insight into the activities and methods of a busy and important coroner's jurisdiction. It was shortly after this, in late 1938, that I learned that there was a vacancy for a coronership in East Surrey. I did not for one moment think that I would be appointed to this vacancy, but in a rather unenthusiastic and unhopeful way I sent in an application. Rather to my astonishment, I found myself appointed. I hesitated as to whether or not I should take the appointment, but after some thought I felt that I should do so.

My predecessor as coroner in Surrey, Dr. Lord, had indirectly and involuntarily produced a change in the law. He had held an inquest on a person killed by a motor car on the Kingston By-Pass Road. There was nothing very unusual about this. What was unusual was that the car was driven by Lord de Clifford. The Kingston inquest jury took the rather narrow and perhaps parochial view that one could not allow these — (unprintable) Lords to mow down the local citizens, and promptly brought in a verdict of manslaughter. This meant a full dress trial of Lord de Clifford before his robed peers in the House of Lords.

Sir Henry Curtis-Bennet, K.C., who defended his lordship, had no difficulty in obtaining a verdict of "Not guilty". But it was recognised following this case that this procedure was somewhat archaic, and it was abolished by Act of Parliament; now peers of the realm have to meet charges in the ordinary courts, like the rest of us.

Like nearly all new appointees, I thought it right to introduce what I felt were some necessary changes in the existing practice in the Surrey coroner's area. These changes did not necessarily make for my popularity; but then, I reflected wryly, a coroner has no particular right to expect to be popular. He is, after all, dealing with tragic and unexpected deaths; deaths in which many different people may ultimately have different and conflicting interests.

One of the difficulties that I encountered in Surrey was the question of my staff. In London and other large centres it has long been the practice that the coroner's officers – the officers who deal with the practical aspect of the work, the interviewing of relatives, the taking of statements from witnesses, the arrangements for disposal of the body, and many other sometimes anxious duties – should be serving police officers. This obviously has considerable advantages, and was certainly a practice which commended itself to me. I found that in Surrey this was not the practice. The officers that I inherited were not serving police officers, although some were former police officers – alas, sometimes, past their best years.

I was very anxious to put things on a better basis, and for this purpose had several discussions with the then Chief Constable of Surrey, Joseph Simpson (later to become Sir Joseph Simpson, Commissioner of Police for the Metropolis). He was most courteous and most helpful, although in the final analysis unwilling to concede my main proposal – the allocation to me of full-time police constables as officers. I pointed out that the existing practice, by which the officer called to a death automatically acted as the officer investigating for me had disadvantages: not only was he likely to be a junior and inexperienced man in police matters generally, but he would almost certainly be very inexperienced in coroner's cases; this might well be the first (and perhaps only) coroner's case he would ever deal with. Simpson was studiously polite and sympathetic to my point of view, but he was clearly unwilling to yield any units of his already undermanned force to me. Later, of course, when he became Police Commissioner for the Metropolis, he accepted there the existing practice which he had firmly resisted in Surrey. His successor in the Metropolis, Sir Robert Mark, was clearly a most valuable addition to the upper echelons of the police, and obviously a man of action with progressive views.

Those who know the workings of the coroner system will know that it revolves around the activities of the pathologist whom the coroner instructs and pays (from public funds); it is the pathologist who after post-mortem examination will certify the cause of death, provide details which may assist in identification, estimate the level of any poison or alcohol in the body at the time of death, say whether, for example, a body found in the river died from drowning, or was already dead from other causes when thrown in the river (in this event no water will have been inhaled into the lungs). The pathologist's examination will provide much other essential and valuable information.

I have had a number of pathologists who have given me much and most valuable help, and to whom I am most grateful. It was the late Sir Bentley Purchase who used to say that it took an honest pathologist to say that he was unable to give the cause of death. He, of course, was the well known North London coroner. But this does sometimes happen, and in these cases it is quite proper for the coroner to certify that death is due to "causes unascertainable".

I am dealing now with a far from amusing subject, and I am reminded of two pathologist's cases. In one of these cases, the local country police had, on my instructions, called out a busy pathologist to the mortuary to do a post-mortem examination. But ignoring the standing instructions, and indeed ignoring commonsense, they had omitted to move the body to the mortuary. The pathologist, on his arrival, was not unnaturally annoyed and perhaps bad tempered, and he proceeded to tell the police what he thought of them, his language including the use of, among others, the word "bloody". This resulted in my receiving a long typewritten account and complaint by the police of the pathologist's behaviour and his language. I managed to suppress my astonishment that the pathologist's language was of a kind unfamilar to the police, and wrote to them that I thought that the pathologist was perfectly right. I heard no more of the matter.

In another case the dismembered pieces of a decapitated woman were found in two suitcases. The pathologist's written report described these appalling mutilations, and then added in a final paragraph: "In my opinion the deceased had not been interfered with."

I recall – since we are talking about the disagreeable subject of dismembered bodies – an occasion when my wife and I were being entertained to dinner by the late Professor Francis Camps. At this time he was very much occupied with the case of Stanley Setty, whose dismembered corpse had been found off the Essex marshes. Camps, with his enormous and ebullient enthusiasm, insisted on showing us the somewhat grim and macabre photographs in this case. My wife felt considerable distaste and repugnance at these. I myself, well aware of her lack of enthusiasm for exhibits of this kind, had always made it a practice not to leave similar photographs about the house, but later the excellent dinner, wine and conversation dispelled her symptoms.

I became involved in a somewhat controversial matter quite early in my days as a coroner. A coroner of course occupies a judical office, if a minor one. He has to act judicially in the cases which he has to investigate. But of course he can only act in these cases if he knows about them, that is to say he can only act if someone tells him about them. I found that the law and practice with regard to reporting deaths to the coroner by doctors (who were obviously the people in the best position to do so) varied enormously.

In order that the appropriate deaths should be consistently and duly reported to me, I sent a letter to all the hospitals in my jurisdiction requesting that these deaths should be reported to me, and relying for my legal authority for this request on what I described as a "common law" duty on the part of the doctors to do so. This request by me was not altogether favourably received by some doctors, who would naturally prefer not to report a case to the coroner, but merely to issue a death certificate. There was clearly a conflict here, and the British Medical Association quite properly took the opinion of counsel upon the matter. The law, as is known, moves slowly, but I was glad after some months to learn that counsel had advised that I was quite right, and that there was a common law duty on the part of doctors to report deaths to the coroner.

But clearly some doctors were dissatisfied with the opinion that they had received. The matter moved into the hands of one of the medical defence societies; they took the opinion of another counsel who came forward with another opinion that pleased them much more: counsel said that there was no such duty at common law. But whatever the strict legal position, cases continued to be reported to me, and I had more than enough work to do. Nevertheless, there was obviously an area here of possible doubt and possible conflict.

A coroner's duties necessarily bring him into contact with many medical questions, and into relationship with the medical profession. Since the only cases with which the coroner deals are fatal ones and cases which have gone wrong, this may give the coroner a quite distorted view of medical practice, and fail to give him an insight into the vast majority of cases in which medical treatment can have a happy result. Some, although not all, doctors fail to see that the coroner is in a quasi-judicial position in that it is his clear duty to investigate as fully as he can, and as is reasonable in the circumstances. I found myself in particularly difficult and deep waters with some general practitioners who practised a great deal of major surgery and who did not appreciate my enquiries into those cases that ended fatally. So much was this so, that a formal letter of complaint about me was sent to the British Medical Association; it was also later conveyed to me through an intermediary that Dr. Charles (now Lord) Hill, then Secretary of the British Medical Association would be willing to discuss the matter with me. I am slightly ashamed to say that my first reaction was to feel that this was none of the British Medical Association's business, and to incline to refuse to meet their representative. Second, and perhaps wiser, thoughts however prevailed, and I duly met Dr. Hill. Dr. Hill, who appeared to me to have a wider and more reasonable appreciation of the situation than his colleagues, listened to me carefully and attentively, and finally said: "Your arguments are devastating." It appeared that I had not entirely lost my small skill in advocacy, and I heard no more of this particular matter.

I usually tried to avoid any approach before an inquest to me personally by any interested party who might be anxious to Influence the verdict. Indeed, generally such an approach would be improper. The avoidance of such approaches was sometimes difficult, particularly in the case of the police with whom one was necessarily in contact, since they, the police, were making the necessary enquiries on behalf of the coroner. I recall one case in which an infant's body was found on some waste ground; the circumstances were such that to describe them under the heading of "foul play" would be an understatement. The detective in charge of the case accosted me before the inquest, and deferentially suggested that a suitable verdict might be that the child had not had a separate existence from the mother (if not having had it, obviously its existence could not have been terminated by any act, criminal or otherwise). I had to point out that an objection to this most charitable view of the case was that the infant was wearing a complete hand-knitted jacket and leggings, a rather unusual costume for an infant emerging from the womb. The inquest was adjourned in order that the police might make further enquiries.

Much of my area included a long stretch of the River Thames. Bodies were not infrequently recovered from the river. The first difficulty was identification – who were they. Sometimes dental details provided the answer. A chart of the condition of the teeth might be circulated among dentists and be recognised – it sometimes happened that a dentist would actually recognise his own work. As I have indicated already, not all bodies dragged from the Thames had died from drowning. A body having died from some other cause (possibly criminal) might have been simply dumped in the river. Here the pathologist could be of great help; in drowning cases there is inhalation of water into the lungs; those already dead from other causes before immersion in the water would not show evidence of inhalation of water.

One of the excellent and capable pathologists who did work for me was Dr. Eric Gardner, who had come to coroner's work after many years in general practice. He was a great friend of Sir Bernard Spilsbury, who had earlier dominated the forensic medicine and medico-legal field. Dr. Gardner was very able and full of enthusiasm. It was of Dr. Gardner that one of my officers said: "Dr. Gardner?" "Why 'ed as soon do a post-mortem as 'ave 'is breakfast." Dr. Gardner was the observant pathologist in the "Chalkpit" murder case to which I refer elsewhere in this volume.

I heard the late Lord Goddard, Lord Chief Justice, tell an amusing after-dinner story. I should add that it was told at a dinner of the Coroners' Society – an occasion when what some of us regard as amusing might not be universally regarded in the same light. It was about a disreputable character who earned a precarious living as a racing tipster. His dead body was recovered from the Thames, and was removed to the mortuary for identification. I ought to add that his tips were not generally thought to be good. It so happened that the mortuary at the time housed a number of other bodies. One of the tipster's friends was taken there to identify formally the deceased. A body was produced and shown to the potential witness of identification. "No!, he said, "that ain't him." A second body was then brought forward. Again he said: "No! That ain't him." An attempt was made with a third body. "No, no," he said, "That ain't him either. Just like old Bill. Never in the first three."

Later I found myself involved in what became known as the towpath murder case. Two young girls were missing; in the well-known phrase which all police officers like to use, foul play was suspected. At first only one body was recovered from the Thames, in that part of the river which was in my jurisdiction. At this time Detective Chief Superintendent Herbert Hannam, a most capable and impressive figure, who was in charge of the police enquiries, came to see me with a request: this was that if the other body were found elsewhere in some other coroner's jurisdiction, would I, with the consent of the other coroner, and in order to avoid duplication of the enquiries, agree to accept the second body into my jurisdiction. (The movement, if desired, of bodies in this way is allowed by the law if both coroners agree.) I at once agreed, but in fact that particular problem did not arise, because the second body was later recovered from the Thames within my area. Ultimately there were convictions for murder in respect of both bodies.

Many popular misconceptions exist about coroners and their activities. Many believe that all a coroner has to do is to sit in a well-appointed court two or three times a week, perhaps deliver himself occasionally of material likely to make the evening newspaper headlines, and then retire home and put his feet up. Nothing could be farther from the truth, certainly not in the case of a coroner with a busy jurisdiction. It is not generally appreciated that the greater part of a coroner's work is not done in court at all. Non-inquest cases, that is, cases dealt with by the coroner after post-mortem examination or enquiry only, constitute something like four out of every five cases he deals with. All these non-inquest cases take up a great deal of time before they can be finally disposed of by the coroner. The coroner is one of the few people who can truthfully say that he is on duty for twenty-four hours each day. At any moment he must be available to give a decision: relatives wish to know whether they can go ahead with arrangements for burial or cremation, and for what date. Some relatives, from time to time, wish to remove a body for burial out of England; for this there is a special procedure; only the coroner can authorise this, and he must be available in order to give a decision.

Of course many of the decisions one was called upon to make could be made on the telephone. I have never been fond of this valuable and necessary instrument; indeed, I used to feel very vulnerable at times because of it. I am thinking in particular of one morning when the telephone bell woke me from my sleep at about two or three in the morning. An unidentified male voice told me that he was "coming over to do me". In view of this elegant threat, I politely asked him who he was, but got no name from him. The conversation ended shortly after that, except for the caller's somewhat strange observation to me that "All you medical tribe are the same". I may say that I did not sleep at all well after this. I was puzzled as to who the caller might have been. But in the morning, with perhaps a rather clearer head, I suddenly thought that I knew. I had recently dealt with (as a non-inquest case) the death of a woman at a local hospital. This turned out to be a perfectly natural death, but I knew that the husband of the dead woman was making all sorts of wild and unfounded allegations against the hospital staff. (I did not know this at the time, otherwise I would have ventilated all this at an inquest.) Somehow I had an instinct that this was my telephone caller of the previous night. As I was later to discover, the hospital in order to rid themselves of the complaints against THEIR staff, had given him my telephone number, which was in fact ex-directory. I did not relish the idea of having to take further calls of this kind, and thought it expedient to consult the head of the local C.I.D. I explained, very courageously, that I personally did not mind calls of this kind, but that there were women in the house, and that it was very upsetting for them. The detective superintendent seemed to understand the position. We both agreed that I could not prove who the caller was, and he said that he would let me know later what transpired.

He told me within a few days that when one of his officers called at the address of the man I suspected, he was told that the man was not at home, but would be found in the telephone box across the road. The police were particularly interested in this piece of information, not because of me, but because they had had complaints of a different kind of call – those offensive to women – coming from the same box. But, in the end, our man completely denied, as one would expect, having telephoned me at all. If he was the original caller, as I firmly believe, the police interest in him was sufficient to curtail his activities. I received no more calls from this source.

One cannot be unaware that there has been in the past much criticism of the coroner system. My own view may be partial, but it is that it is essential to have some system by which sudden, unexpected, or violent deaths are investigated by an independent authority. In England and Wales this is done by the coroner's investigation. In Scotland it is done by the Procurator-Fiscal. In the United States, the system varies. Some states have the British coroner system, which they have adopted, although the qualifications there of some coroners leave much to be desired; in other States, like New York City, the system is of the medical examiner, who corresponds to our pathologist, but who also has the power to make the ultimate decision to dispose of the case finally and make further enquiry unnecessary.

A death I investigated – the "chalkpit murder" case, attracted some attention. A man was found strangled by a rope round his neck. His position on the ground was consistent with his having fallen there after death by hanging, the rope having later slipped off, or broken from, the tree above. The local police were quite content to treat the case as one of suicide, but my shrewd and observant pathologist, Dr. Eric Gardner, noticed that whereas the *Locus in quo* consisted of very thick mud, the man's shoes were perfectly clean and beautifully polished. Dr. Gardner concluded that the death had taken place elsewhere, and the body planted where it was found. I gratefully adopted this view and persuaded the reluctant police to make further enquiries. These resulted in three men being charged with murder before Lord Goddard, Lord Chief Justice, one of these, paradoxically, was Mr. Ley, former Australian Minister of Justice. He was sent to Broadmoor because of his mental condition, and died there a year later; the fate of the other two I do not now recall. But at least on this occasion the office of coroner had justified itself.

The recent Brodrick Committee has investigated and considered the coroner system in Great Britain. Following this, the Home Secretary (as I write now in 1975) has announced that he proposes to introduce new legislation, the main effect of which will be to reduce the number of inquests by giving the coroner a very wide discretion to dispense with holding an inquest except in a small number of cases in which an inquest will still be compulsory. Few coroners, it is thought, will have any objection to this. But it does seem to me, if this legislation is passed, that the discretion not to hold an inquest will be exercised by different coroners in different ways; in given sets of circumstances one coroner will hold an inquest, another will not.

Criticism of the coroner's court is sometimes made on the ground that there is no appeal from the verdict of a coroner's court, and that its proceedings are arbitrary. This is true only in the most literal sense of the word "appeal". But an interested party can apply to the High Court for an order that the coroner's (or his jury's) verdict be quashed and a new inquest held by another coroner. Such applications have been made in respect of my court's verdicts on two occasions only in thirty years; both applications failed. One was the Woolf case, to which I refer elsewhere in this book. The other was that of a married woman who, following the birth of a child, was in a room on one of the upper floors of a hospital. She was in a very depressed condition. During the absence of a nurse she was found, having sustained fatal injuries, on the ground floor below her window. The window, a sash-type one, was only slightly open at the bottom, and in my view it would have taken a conscious and deliberate effort for a heavily built woman, which she was, to get out. There was medical evidence that she was a potentially suicidal patient, and that suicidal intent was the most likely explanation of what had happened. The verdict was suicide. The relatives did not like the verdict of suicide, and applied to the Divisional Court to quash it. Leave for this was refused, and a further application was made to the Court of Appeal. The Court of Appeal granted the application, and the case was therefore heard by the Court of Appeal itself. I was intrigued to hear one of the learned Lords of Appeal criticise my wording of the inquest finding that she had "projected herself" from the window; he preferred the more neutral phrase that she had "defenestrated" herself. It did not matter, because the Court agreed that my verdict should remain undisturbed.

The outbreak of war in September, 1939, produced for me, as for other coroners, new and additional problems. The black-out provided its own toll of different and additional road traffic casualties. In their preparations in advance for the war that everyone latterly had realised was inevitable, the Home Office had envisaged civilian casualties in this country on a scale which, fortunately, never occurred. Because of this, deaths due to war injuries, although clearly not natural deaths, were made non-reportable to the coroner. The appropriate regulations, drawn up by the Home Office, made the records and certificates of the mortuary keeper sufficient evidence of the war death. There was a place for the coroner, however. In cases in which it was clear that, although no body was ever recovered, it was evident that the deceased died by enemy action, the coroner was empowered to hold an inquest (in this case, unusually, without a body) and record a verdict that death had occurred and was due to war injuries. Such a case, for example, might be that in which a large bomb fell on a building, destroying and scattering in small pieces – and beyond all recognition – the building and all those known to have been within it at the time. Of course one had to be particularly careful before recording a verdict in these circumstances that a particular person had in fact died of anything; it was not unknown, rarely, for the person whom the coroner had decided was dead to turn up very much alive, and to produce thereby additional problems which had to be cleared. Incidentally, during the war coroners were empowered to sit without juries; I do not recall that this reduced our efficiency.

On many occasions I found myself sitting in court holding inquests, whilst bombs exploded outside with great violence and noise. It was difficult to continue the proceedings as if nothing unusual were happening, but in general we did.

An interesting result of war conditions in England was the very distinct and undoubted fall in the rate of suicides. I was very impressed with this, and considered what possible reason could account for it. I can only think that it was because, in peacetime, many suicides result from an abnormal and disturbed state of mind, often resulting in or resting on some quite marked interference and misdirection of the mental processes and intellect. Once the nation was struggling with great determination against the very real problems and affairs of modern warfare, in other words once the people had something real and positive to fight against and deal with, the lesser psychological disturbances which might otherwise have resulted in suicide receded into the background.

It is remarkable to what lengths relatives will go to attempt to resist a verdict of suicide – even in those cases in which all the evidence points in this direction. The mere tearing-up and destruction of a suicide note in the deceased's handwriting is one of the least of what can be done. An attempt to get a verdict of suicide quashed by the Divisional Court or the Court of Appeal is another step occasionally taken. Because such a step may involve the coroner in additional work, anxiety, and expense, some more cautious coroners have adopted the expedient of the so-called "open" verdict in cases which they believe to be suicide, simply as a form of self-protection.

There were a good many Canadian military units stationed in my district. One road death was that of a pedestrian who was struck and killed by a Canadian military vehicle during the black-out. The vehicle had been driven by a private, who was accompanied by an officer passenger. I duly held the inquest. There was no evidence of reckless or criminal negligence, and the verdict was one of accidental death.

I heard nothing more about this case until some months later, when information reached me that the evidence given at the inquest had been untrue. It had been the officer driving, and the private a passenger. Further, the officer (and not, so far as I remember, the private) was to be charged by court-martial with perjury. Still more, in order to sustain a charge of perjury, my evidence as to what had happened at the inquest was essential. I was not at all anxious to attend the court-martial, and pointed out that my wartime petrol allowance would not extend to take me to Sussex, where the court-martial was to be held. This was of no avail to me, because the Canadians promptly undertook to collect me in a jeep and transport me to Sussex. And on the appropriate day, the jeep drew up at my house. I was asked, before taking my seat in it, to sign a form which entirely exonerated the Canadian authorities in the event of my suffering any injury. I obviously could have refused to sign this, but, perhaps rashly, I did. The military driver was not the most cautious of men, and we had some hair-raising moments on our way. I was entertained most regally at lunch, being seated next to the General. I remember my very strong impression that the Canadian Army's food was very much better than that of us poor civilians; perhaps it was right that it should be so. I gave evidence as to what had occurred at the inquest. I was then cross-examined by the defending officer, who appeared to be very able and had evolved a rather ingenious defence. He suggested to me that it did not matter, for the purposes of the inquest, who was driving, and that my verdict would have been the same in either event. I thought at first that I would have to agree with this novel proposition, but a little reflection showed that he was wrong. Among the details which, understandably, the coroner has to ascertain and record for the verdict is the identity of the driver. I made it clear that I did not accept the defending officer's proposition, but I understood later that the officer had been found guilty of the offence charged, although I believe that the penalty imposed was not a severe one.

We had all been accustomed to what were called the V-Ones, the so-called buzz bombs, whose engines used to cut out before the explosion took place. But I had the doubtful privilege of having the first V-Two – the very much larger rocket bomb which landed and exploded without any warning – explode within my "manor" in the vicinity of Richmond, Surrey. At the time there was a considerable air of mystery as to what precisely had happened. I was not told anything officially about this matter – and indeed this was right if any deaths so caused were deaths due to war injury. There were, of course, considerable casualties, and there were rumours locally of gas mains having exploded, and various other hypotheses were advanced. It was only some time later that I learnt what had happened. It so happened that at about this time (1944) I was a patient in a London hospital, and the patient in the next room was a very important man from Fleet Street. Within minutes of our hearing an explosion, he would have heard from his colleagues on his bedside telephone exactly where the bomb had been, and what the degree of damage was.

In quite another connection, I recall, in my innocence, being somewhat shocked and surprised when a prominent Whitehall official telephoned me to ask me to leave out the address of the premises of a friend of his in which a death had occurred upon which I was holding an inquest. I told him quite firmly, that I could not do this, but I found that my confidence in some aspects of our governmental departments was somewhat shaken.

It quite often happened that members of Parliament, quite properly, would write to me on a constituent's behalf, because the constituent felt that something I had done or said was wrong; sometimes it was the verdict which was disputed. I usually found that the understandably bereaved relative (and hence his member of Parliament) had completely mis-understood or misconstrued some event, and I always found that the member of Parliament was agreeably willing to be informed by me of the real position, and was quite satisfied when so informed.

The question of suicide is frequently a painful one. Often relatives are reluctant to admit that their lamented and loved ones could have chosen this deliberate act. Sometimes their objection results from religious or sentimental grounds. Sometimes it rests on the existence of a life insurance policy, upon which payment will not be made in the event of suicide.

Suicide by overdose of some sleeping tablets has become common, almost fashionable, and tending to replace the older fashioned suicide by coal gas poisoning. Again in these cases efforts are frequently made to try to avoid a suicide verdict. Of course if the deceased leaves a suicide note in his own handwriting, there can be no doubt. I think it likely, in some cases, that such notes are destroyed or concealed.

Some doctors have advanced the theory that after taking a normal dose of sleeping tablets, the patient may become confused and take a further dose, amounting to a lethal dose. It is difficult to reconcile this evidence with that of the pathologist, who may well find that something like fifty tablets (instead of the normal two tablets) have been taken at one time. The taking of such a massive overdose can only be consistent, one would think, with a deliberate and voluntary act.

Until the Suicide Act of 1961, suicide was a crime – *felo de se.* It is still a crime to counsel or to procure the suicide of another. I myself would be very much in favour of holding inquests in private in suicide cases – with perhaps a public announcement of what the verdict is. Indeed such a course would be within the discretion of coroners which seems likely to be included in any new legislation. I do not see the value of publicity of the evidence in these cases; it is distressing to the relatives, and some think that further suicides are provoked by those who are inclined to imitate that which they read. But, subject to what I have just said, there is much to be said in favour of a public hearing of the evidence in the general run of cases heard by the coroner, as against a merely private hearing. Publicity, after all, should dispel rumour, gossip, and untruth. Further, there is ample opportunity at the inquest for interested persons to hear and question the evidence, some of which may be of vital importance later in questions of civil liability, compensation, probate, and assurance policies; hence the fact that the inquest is frequently the happy hunting ground of solicitors and members of the Bar who are seeking, quite properly and rightly, to gain and assess material which may be of value in later proceedings.

One aspect of the work of a coroner is his position in relation to deaths resulting from aircraft accidents. Of course it is his duty to hold inquests into such deaths. But in the case of multiple deaths resulting from an aircraft disaster on a large scale, a full public enquiry is usually held, with all possible technical and other evidence fully available and given. In these circumstances, the usual course taken by the coroner is to await the outcome of the public enquiry, in order to avoid duplication of investigation, and then resume his inquest later in the light of what is then known. But in the case of deaths resulting from accidents to light aircraft, where usually and fortunately the death toll is much lighter, no public enquiry is held. I was a witness at the enquiry which was set up by the Government into the procedure for investigating aircraft accidents, and I did my best to make the point that in the case of these smaller disasters the coroner's inquest offered to the bereaved relatives the only opportunity they had to hear the evidence of what had happened. I was glad to see, when the Committee (presided over by Mr., now Lord Justice, Cairns) reported, that they said that they were impressed with this point, and that the Committee had no doubt that the Coroner's traditional freedom of action should stand.

On a lighter vein (if such is possible in this context) I recall an inquest on a body which had been recovered from the Thames. The circumstances suggested a possible suicide. After various formal witnesses, including one of identification, a very young C.I.D. officer went into the witness box, gave some important and necessary evidence, and then ended his evidence by saying that the deceased was in no financial difficulty and that his bank account showed a "very healthy" balance. I concluded this case, and then went on to begin another.

Something must have stirred uneasily at the back of my mind, and perhaps somewhat irregularly at that stage I asked my officer to get hold of, if he could, the bank statement. This was then produced, and I found that the "healthy balance" was large, and in red figures – the deceased owed a lot of money to his bank. I thought this fact sufficiently important, even at that stage, for a correction to be made in open court, and I did this.

My relations with the press were generally good, although there were obviously good and not so good reporters. My initials happen to be C. F. When however, one local newspaper persisted in reporting these as B. F. I felt that something should be done. I wrote a semi-humorous letter to the editor on which I said that I quite understood how I might be regarded by the reporter, but I suggested a little more accuracy in the reports. My letter was taken in good part, apologies were tendered, and all went well afterwards.

The coroner's court, with its association with death, tragedy, and human unhappiness, is not the place where one would normally expect anything even remotely humorous to occur, but certain "near misses" come to mind. At one inquest, counsel who appeared for an interested party asked if he could be permitted to call an expert witness. I readily agreed, and this gentleman went into the witness box. Counsel then asked him, in the brisk and confident manner that counsel do, if he was Mr. — and if his address was —. Answer: "Yes." Counsel then went on: "I think that you are a chartered engineer and a Fellow of the Royal Institute of British Architects". Answer: "No." I found myself muttering, as I thought *sotto voce*, "One is reminded of Failed B.A. Cantab." The sharp ears of the reporter in court, however, heard what I said and there was an amusing reference to it in the next issue of the local newspaper. The reference was, of course, to the aspiring gentleman from India whose visiting cards were inscribed with these magic words.

On another occasion, in a traffic case, a witness went into the box, and having given his name and address embarked in a dull monotonous and mechanical tone in a long recitation which went something like this: "On Monday September 3rd at about ten-thirty in the morning I was walking along Royal Avenue in an easterly direction on the left hand side of the road. Coming towards me was a Morris Minor motor car, red in colour, driven by a man in chauffeur's uniform . . ." and so it went on and on, in a flat monotone. Eventually, having told his tale, he stopped. There was something about the way in which he said all this which prompted me to do something which I have never done before or since. I said to him: "When did you learn that by heart?" He answered: "Yesterday, Sir." Of course, provided that his evidence was true, there is no valid reason why he should not have learnt it by heart. But giving evidence in this way has its disadvantages, and is not to be recommended.

At about this time, I was a member of a deputation of representatives of coroners who saw at the Home Office the then Home Secretary, Major Gwilym Lloyd George (later Lord Tenby), on a matter which was causing us some concern. We had a very courteous and attentive reception, and the Home Secretary was good enough to say that our arguments were "crystal clear". None the less, nothing was done, so far as I know, about this particular problem; but such are the ways of government and of government departments.

It was at about this time, in 1960, that I became involved in a case which was generally referred to at the time as "the Woolf case", and which later developed into a High Court action which rejoiced in the somewhat forbidding and intimidating title of "Woolf v. Baron and others". The "others" included the Commissioner of Police for the Metropolis.

Herman Woolf was a gentleman who had been knocked down by a known motor car, a Jaguar, in Park Lane, London. There were a number of witnesses as to this, including the driver of the car. There was no suggestion of reckless or criminal negligence on the part of the driver of the car. After being knocked down, Mr. Woolf was taken to St. George's Hospital, where he was seen by a number of doctors. An X-ray of his skull was taken, but this disclosed no fracture. He was conscious, and no serious injuries were thought to be present. The hospital accordingly discharged him. The police, however, had other views, because Mr. Woolf had been found to have in his possession a quantity of cannabis, or Indian hemp. The police, therefore, took him into custody, and he was placed in a detention room at West End Central Police Station and charged. He had had, in fact, two previous convictions for possession of this drug.

Within the next days, Mr. Woolf began to develop signs and symptoms of brain injury; he was taken back to St. George's Hospital where he was again seen by doctors (at least one of whom had seen him on his earlier visit to the hospital), his changed and worsened condition was recognised, and he was taken the next day to a neurosurgical hospital in Wimbledon (at that time within my jurisdiction). There his condition gradually deteriorated, and in spite of appropriate treatment he died there another eleven days later.

The circumstances were duly reported to me and it was clearly my duty to hold an inquest; so far as I knew the facts this appeared to be a not unusual case of a pedestrian having died from injuries sustained whilst in collision with a motor car; in such cases the coroner is bound to summon a jury, and this was duly done.

The inquest was held before me and the jury, and the verdict (not of me, but of the jury, although I fully agreed with it) was that Mr. Woolf had died of the injuries received when he came into collision with the motor car, and that his death was accidental.

It was many weeks before I heard anything more about this case. Then odd paragraphs began to appear in some of the less reputable organs of the Press, hinting that Mr. Woolf had not died from any injuries caused by a motor car; no, suggested they, might not these injuries more probably have been caused when he was detained in a police cell? The fact that there was no evidence of this and that the death had been fully and publicly investigated seemed to be immaterial.

It was soon after this that I received a number of communications from the late Mr. Sydney Silverman, M.P., a solicitor, and a doughty fighter in some lost causes. I must say that his letters to me were couched in unnecessarily unfriendly, and even derogatory, terms. Mr. Silverman had not attended the inquest, and I duly supplied him with a copy of the evidence. He intimated that he was acting for the relatives, and that he would be applying to the High Court to have the inquisition quashed, in effect applying for an order to set the inquest proceedings and verdict aside, and to ask for a new inquest – clearly one to be held by another coroner.

While all this was going on, a motor car presented itself at my front door at home one day. Two men dismounted from it, and having managed to get me to my front door, they announced themselves as being reporters from one of the less esteemed journals of Fleet Street, and proceeded to question me about the Woolf case. I made it clear that I did not propose to discuss the matter with them, and I was having a little difficulty in persuading them to leave the premises. Suddenly a third man, who must have been lying hidden on the floor at the back of the car, got up and pointed a camera at me. I threatened him and his newspaper with the most dire legal proceedings if they should publish the photograph. They did not publish it. I should add that, during these happenings at the house, our Swiss au pair of that time was terrified at what was going on, and must have realised that some somewhat unfriendly men were being interviewed at the door.

But to return to a more solid threat, Mr. Silverman. I decided to consult an old friend of mine, Sir Sidney Littlewood, a solicitor and former President of the Law Society. At this state I did not know, although I had a fair idea, what Mr. Silverman was alleging.

In due course we received, in writing, the grounds upon which Mr. Silverman was seeking to set the jury's verdict aside, and of course the suggestion had now been firmly made that Mr. Woolf's injuries had been caused, not by a motor car, but by the police.

Sir Sidney Littlewood got busy with the preparation of my case. Curiously enough Sir Sidney's brother-in-law, Lord Brain, was a famous neurologist. Although I did not know it at the time, Sir Sidney had obtained a written opinion from Lord Brain on the medical aspects of the case. Lord Brain's report was to the effect that the Woolf history was the not uncommon one of a man being injured and showing no immediate signs of brain injury at all, and thereafter as intracranial pressure from brain damage builds up, symptoms and signs only then becoming manifest for the first time. (X-Ray pictures are frequently negative in such cases).

Unfortunately, for technical legal reasons relating to the law of evidence, we were unable to use Lord Brain's opinion in the subsequent proceedings.

The case duly came up for hearing before the Divisional Court in the Strand before Lord Parker, Lord Chief Justice, Mr. Justice (later Lord Justice) Winn, and Mr. Justice Fenton Atkinson. I was ably represented by Mr. Peter Bristow, of Counsel (later Mr. Justice Bristow).

One of the points in the evidence which seemed to me to be vital was that when Mr. Woolf was taken back to St. George's Hospital for the second time (that is, after police custody), one of the doctors who then saw him was one of the doctors who had seen him on the earlier occasion at hospital, before police custody. This doctor was quite clear that there were no additional injuries to be seen on the second attendance.

There was also a curious moment during the proceedings in the High Court which impressed itself on my mind. It appeared in the hospital notes taken on the first visit. There is a test of brain injury, which consists in tickling the patient's foot. If the big toe bends down, all is well. If it goes up, this suggests brain damage or brain malfunction. In Mr. Woolf's case, the big toe had gone upwards on the first visit. When evidence was given of this being recorded on the hospital notes on the first visit, it was enormously encouraging to hear Mr. Justice Winn say: "O, yes. Babinski." For the benefit of the uninitiated, I must add that this test and its sign are known as "Babinski's sign", after the doctor who first observed it. It was clear that in the case of at least one judge, Mr. Justice Winn, who had been listening most patiently and attentively without so far intervening, the point had made its mark (and indeed was familiar to him, no doubt from the many road traffic injury cases that he had dealt with when at the Bar).

In a sense, it was fortunate for me that the main attack was directed against the police, whose counsel, Mr. Leonard, dealt very effectively with the somewhat shaky allegations on the other side. Indeed, towards the end of the case Lord Parker indicated that there was no need for Mr. Bristow, my counsel to address the court. The Woolf case was at an end, and the court refused to grant the order which Mr. Silverman had sought, through counsel, to obtain.

Some time afterwards the Home Secretary set up an enquiry into the actions of the Metropolitan Police in relation to Mr. Woolf. This enquiry was held by Mr. Norman (later Sir Norman, Director of Public Prosecutions) Skelhorn. This enquiry took evidence in much more detail and from many more witnesses (seventy-seven in fact) than either I or the High Court had ever received, and firmly announced its conclusion among other things, that the police had acted perfectly properly, and that no police action had played any part in this death. It is of interest also that the expert neuro-surgical evidence at the enquiry confirmed my own view that there was a fracture of the skull and damage to the brain in existence on the occasion of the first visit to hospital, immediately following the collision. The expert evidence was also that the failure to recognise the seriousness of this condition earlier did not prejudice Mr. Woolf's chances of recovery.

* * *

We had a succession of Swiss au pairs – girls – in the house who were usually sturdy and sensible young women. But occasionally some examples of their fractured English caused us some amusement. Once, on returning home, I asked the au pair whether there had been any telephone messages for me. She said there had. She said "Coroner England" had telephoned to speak to me. I was mystified, and assumed that she had made a mistake in the name. The only person, I thought, who could have fitted this title would have been Sir Bentley Purchase – and he certainly would not have been averse to assuming such a title. A later telephone call, however, made it clear that he girl was absolutely right. The call had been from Mr. England, Coroner for Great Yarmouth. By some extraordinary set of circumstances a body had been hovering between his jurisdiction and mine; we were able quite amicably and happily to reach an agreement about this which solved the difficulty. This sort of situation is more common in adjoining coroners' jurisdictions; the law solves this by permitting coroners anywhere to agree the transfer of a body from one area to another.

At home, we once suffered a plumbing disaster – a burst pipe or some similar catastrophe. As is well known, *l'Anglais avec son sangfroid habituel* on such occasions resorts to the first line of defence and consolation, which is quite simply a cup of tea. We had done this and had had our first cup, when I became aware of the Swiss girl, clutching the kettle, and wandering about the room in what looked like a state of automatism, muttering: "Perhaps I should make water again".

I tremble to think what malapropisms in foreign tongues I have uttered myself, in my ignorance of these languages. One I do remember is in France when we were in charge of the young French girl courier, who was shepherding us into a bus. I was not sure whether the bus was too full to take us; I asked the girl: *Etes vous pleine?* She looked rather uncomfortable and embarrassed, I thought. Not until a long time afterwards did I discover that colloquially *pleine* can mean pregnant.

But to return to the problems of a coroner. I had a number of mental hospitals within my area. These provided a fertile source of work for me, some of them complicated and difficult. One such was the case reported to me of a frail woman, who had been bodily seized by one of the other female patients and plunged into a bath of boiling water. She had died from the scalds sustained in this way.

I thought it proper to call at the hospital in order to acquire some better knowledge of what had happened. I there saw the medical officer concerned. He told me what he knew about the case. He explained that the assailant – for such she was – had been a very violent and disorientated patient in the hospital for a long time. But, he added, she had had a particular line of treatment (whatever it was that was then in vogue) and that she was very much better because of this. He asked me whether I would like to see the patient. I said that I would, and after a time the lady was brought into the room. The medical officer then addressed her and, indicating me, said: "Just tell the gentleman all about it, and what happened".

The patient then burst into a stream of demented, unintelligible gibberish which continued unabated for some minutes. At the end of this the doctor turned to me and triumphantly said: "You see, she's very much better". I did not see.

There resulted in this case a criminal charge against this patient which, understandably and quite properly, did not produce a conviction. The lady was rightly found unfit to plead.

In 1965, with the reorganisation of the boundaries of local government, I was appointed Coroner for the Western district of Greater London, a jurisdiction which gave me a larger area, together with some of the less desirable areas in London, as it seemed to me. My acquaintance with some of the more sordid and unattractive human activities became more detailed. I was, of course, only involved in a very special and very particular way with the new local authority, the Greater London Council, but I must say that I did not feel that mere massive size, as was the case here, necessarily made for more ease and smoothness in administration.

No one, it is said, is a hero to his own valet. No doubt a similar observation could be made in relation to one's wife. She has gallantly tolerated my idiosyncrasies and my impatience for years. Perhaps this has been in some way related to my changes of profession. She is apt, when pressed by me to give a clear answer to a particular question, to reply, quite simply: "I am not in the witness box now". I am afraid that at this stage I admit my defeat, and withdraw from the contest, although I am sometimes tempted to comment on the workings and lack of logic of the artistic temperament (she having, as a talented artist, interrupted a five years scholarship at the Royal Academy Schools in order to marry me).

An opportunity occurred in 1970 for my wife and I to visit the United States. This was on a house exchange basis which we thought very attractive. In the event we did go to the States, although our hosts there did not come to England because of an eye condition which one of them was unfortunate enough to develop.

Of course all sorts of formalities had to be completed. We joined a crowd of others at the American Embassy in Grosvenor

Square – all of us seeking visas for permission to stay in the States. I could not help contrasting our own carefree state (after all, we were merely seeking a holiday) with those very anxious looking people who presumably wanted something much more: permission to be able to work in the States.

Finally we took off in a Jumbo aircraft from Heathrow. The plane took the polar route; we were looking down on frozen wastes and a lot of ice floes surrounded by black looking water. When I later told my grandsons about flying over the North Pole, they were not at all impressed; I could not help feeling that at their age I would have been, but then I am two generations removed from them.

We did not sleep, although many others, probably seasoned travellers did. We arrived at Los Angeles Airport, there to be interviewed by an immigration officer. He had already dealt with the child in front of us in the queue; he pronounced her to be a "smart cookie". When he came to us, he appeared to consult an enormous black book, which clearly contained the names and personal details of undesirable characters, who were in no circumstances to be admitted. Rather surprisingly, perhaps, our names did not appear to be there. He then asked me a number of questions (my recollection, which may be wrong, is that on the visa application I had already been asked whether I was a member of the Communist party; the answer was no). He finally, and somewhat abruptly, said: "I'll give you six months". Although the resemblance of this to a judicial sentence was too close to be comfortable, I took it that we had passed, and we went through the controls. We had already booked a room at one of the airport hotels, avoiding the town itself because we had been warned of its notorious smog. We found coping with Los Angeles traffic while carrying our suitcases in the darkness rather difficult, but eventually arrived at our hotel, where we spent a comfortable night. By this time, after a long flight, our "time machine", or our ability to distinguish night from day, had almost gone – the familiar "time lag" syndrome.

In the morning I decided to have a bath. This was difficult, indeed I thought impossible. The American tap, a circular object, would not respond to any manoeuvre that I made. I could produce no water from it. I therefore dialled for "room service" and explained my problem. The receptionist was charming, but explained that the plumber would not be on duty for another two hours. But in the meantime, she said, she would send up the boy to see whether he could do anything. "The boy" proved to be a gentleman between seventy and eighty years of age, but he, unlike me, knew the trick of this particular tap. It was quite easy, when you knew, and I got my bath.

Then we went down to the coffee room of the hotel for breakfast. What a delightful experience that was. Coming from a country where standards of service have steadily deteriorated over the years, what a pleasure it was to be served a most appetising and perfectly prepared breakfast by friendly and spotlessly uniformed waitresses, who immediately responded to one's slightest order, indeed anticipated it. We were enchanted with our first impression of the States. This contrasted so much with the service at breakfast time which we knew so well in England – often unwilling, slow, and served, if served at all, by sour-faced and reluctant staff.

We took a short flight to Orange County airport, where our kindly host awaited us. He and his family had, with great hospitality, gone to stay with friends in order to give us the run of their house. This was at Laguna Beach, on the coast between Los Angeles and the Mexican border. We stayed for three weeks at Laguna, and then became independent tourists. At Laguna we used to go out into the garden to pick apricots for our breakfast. Whilst sitting on the verandah we were fascinated to watch the movements of the humming birds; their friends the mocking birds did their utmost to keep us awake at night.

After Laguna, we moved on to San Francisco, rightly described as the most exciting city in the West, with its Golden Gate appearing in the mists, its Chinatown, its Fisherman's Wharf, and Nob Hill, so-called because the wealthy protected their families from the unpleasant docks area by building their great houses on the heights. It was, perhaps, saddening to learn that Californian stockbrokers had to get out of their beds before dawn to be at their desks when the Stock Exchange opens in New York. From San Francisco we joined a coach tour, which was covering other parts of California. We two were the only British on the tour, and attracted some little attention. We found the Americans friendly, hospitable, and kind, but, dare one say it, a few were sometimes a little naive. We also discovered something that I had not previously known, that some very good wines were made in California.

The coach trip was most interesting. Out of previously barren and arid desert, there had been made fertile agricultural land. We admired the ingenious system of irrigation which had been adopted to produce this happy result.

Some of our fellow tourists were very curious about us. There was one gentleman in particular who, whenever the coach stopped, would come up to me and say, in that well-known transatlantic accent which cannot be produced on paper, "What profession did you follow when you were back home?" I, rightly or wrongly, did not think that it would be good for his psychological health if I gave him graphic and macabre details of my grim profession, and politely told him so, but this did not stop his enquiries. The driver of the coach, as is usual on these occasions, constituted himself guide, philosopher and friend to his charges, and he used to talk through a microphone at us. One day he was driving us through various productive areas: apples, pears, plums, figs, melons all flourished. He gave us an elaborate description of how the fig pollen was transferred from male to female flowers by the activities of a very useful beetle. At the next stop I saw difficulties ahead. My fellow passenger came up to me again. "Well," he said to me, "Did you follow the details of the sex life of the fig tree?" Very seriously, and without a smile, I said: "Yes, it had something to do with the fig leaf, didn't it?" "Oh!" he said, "You think it goes back to Biblical times?" "Yes" I said. Then, once more, came the question to me: "What profession did you follow . . . etc.?" I again avoided that one, and he then said: "Well, I think that you are a writer of pornographic novels." Without batting an eyelid, and with an air of great importance, I said: "As a matter of fact, I am Professor Emeritus of Applied Pornography at

Oxford University". My questioner took one look at me, and fled. He did not put his question to me again.

We spent a couple of days at Yosemite National Park – a delightful place where the air was like wine and the bird and animal life most interesting. It was reputed that there were also bears there, but I think that this fable was invented merely so that the coach driver could give us a jocular instruction. If we were chased by a bear, he said, we were not to rush to the coach; he said that the drivers of these had been instructed not to allow aboard the coach any lady running with a bear behind. We all dutifully laughed.

We also visited and stayed at Monterey, associated with John Steinbeck and Cannery Row, Cannery Row now is a rather run-down and seedy artists' quarter. Robert Louis Stevenson was another who lived in Monterey for a time; we saw an interesting museum and house linked with his stay there.

My description of our visit to the States would not be complete if I did not, once again, refer to the very high standards of service which we met there. At Laguna we had catered and cooked for ourselves, except for those meals which we took in restaurants. Even in the supermarkets, where we did our shopping, there was the utmost politeness. Even when one was performing that sometimes painful act, paying the bill, one was given the farewell words of "Have a good day". One may say that words do not mean a great deal, but we felt that a little of this spirit at home would do no harm.

We did a lot of swimming from the beach at Laguna. Our own view was that the so-called Pacific Ocean is misnamed. It is not pacific at all. An enormous breaker would knock one to the ground, either on entering or on leaving the sea. Just as one picked oneself up and tried to recover one's breath, another breaker would knock one down again – and so it went on. None the less, it was all very enjoyable. We were very impressed with the enormous heat-proof and insulated ice boxes of food which the Americans brought down to the beach. Other interesting local inhabitants were the seals, whose habits and antics were fascinating.

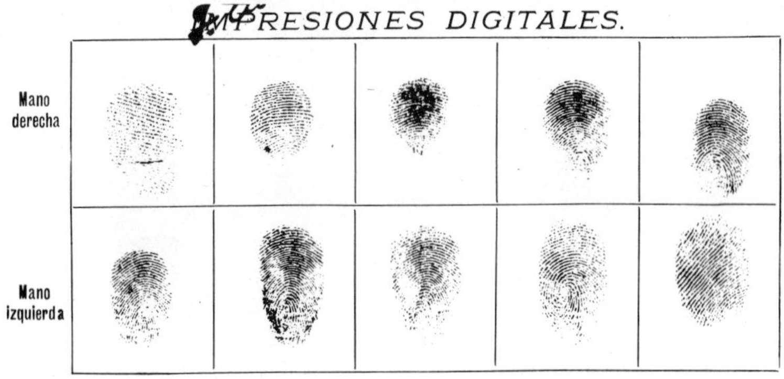

The Ship Surgeon's photograph and finger-prints; taken before his admission to Argentina (1930)

The Ship Surgeon's home for two months

The Author and wife on holiday in Norway
about 1952

The Author and wife picking oranges
in California (1970)

A view of Rio de Janeiro and the Sugar Loaf Mountain (1970)

The Author, wife and daughter in Venice

The Author (foreground)
at a wedding reception

The Author's daughter and son-in-law
in Florence

Chapter 2

Some Short Reflections on the Office of Coroner

My own views on this question may be partial, but when I hear it said that the office of coroner is archaic, and that coroners are anachronisms, I see perfectly well what is meant, and would hesitate to disagree outright. But I do think that some such office is essential; after all, the ascertainment of the exact cause of death is important; upon it may well turn important legal rights and obligations, questions of insurance and inheritance, questions of civil or criminal liability, and many others. Many of the duties of the modern coroner have been inherited from his medieval predecessor.

Certainly some features of the coroner system could hardly be said not to be archaic. The required view of the body by the coroner (not now by the jury) is simply a relic of the days when evidence of injury, and sometimes identity, was obtained in this particular way. Nowadays we have, in any event, the evidence of a highly skilled and experienced pathologist as to the injuries, and evidence of identity by a witness who knew the deceased.

Some critics may say that inquests, for example, on treasure trove are archaic. I have held several very interesting inquests on treasure trove; in these one usually has the expert assistance of highly qualified experts from the British Museum. I remember two small boys who discovered some Roman coins of the reign of Vespasian on Wimbledon Common. I solemnly held an inquest, and the jury decided that the coins were treasure trove. In such cases the practice is that the finder is paid the value of the treasure, which is in turn retained by the British Museum. It is an essential, if this procedure is to be followed, that the finder should have promptly and fully reported his find.

On another occasion there was great excitement because a gold ring was found in Kew Gardens. Was this more treasure trove? I began to make some enquiries, when it suddenly appeared that a lady had lost her ring in the Gardens, and I hastily withdrew from the scene.

My own view of the coroner system remains that it is of essential and great value to the community as a whole. I cannot help being reminded of the petition which was being drafted by the Judges many years ago for presentation to the reigning monarch. It began: "Conscious as we are of our own infirmities". But the shrewd draftsman later altered this to: "Conscious as we are of each other's 'infirmities' ". In the same way, I think that most coroners would readily agree that there are among their brethren some who have almost invited criticism of their ancient and honourable office by the manner in which some cases have been handled; of course this must happen in all professions and in all walks of life. But coroners' inquests in many cases have been of enormous value in directing public or professional attention to specific and potentially fatal hazards in building and engineering operations, in anaesthetic, surgical, and pharmaceutical risks, electrical dangers, and many other fields. It was the inquests of some coroners which first directed attention to the possible risks involved in taking the contraceptive pill – the risk of blood clots forming and becoming detached in the circulation with fatal results. Perhaps this risk is less than it was at first thought to be, but it was the inquest proceedings which first drew attention to it.

The study of the causes of road accidents has been very

much assisted by material derived from inquests; indeed, details of these inquests have been regularly transmitted to the Road Research Laboratory.

It is inevitable that my professional experiences should have led me to some personal views and some broad conclusions on some of the problems and questions with which I have had to deal.

Road traffic fatalities have occupied a good deal of my time. All kinds of theories are proposed with great force (and, no doubt, sincerity) by all kinds of experts.

I, too, have some views. Firstly, whatever anybody may say to the contrary, I am convinced that the speed of the vehicles in the particular situation involved is a much more lethal factor than many would agree. Secondly, one hears the description "woman driver" used with obviously critical and unfavourable intent. My own experience is that on the whole women drivers are good drivers, and when they are good, they are very very good. There is a minority of women drivers who perhaps suffer from an excess of caution; it is possible that sometimes by (not their speed) but by their very slowness and indecision they may lead to a collision, but I repeat that these are in a minority.

Most traffic accidents are caused by a fault or failure in human conduct, whether by a driver or by a pedestrian. The suggestion that many accidents are caused by a faulty vehicle is in my view quite unfounded. In any event, the present Ministry of Transport vehicle test is of very little value, since in it only a few components of the vehicle are required to be examined. Indeed, a former Minister of Transport has described this test as a farce. Its scope is now being enlarged.

Nor am I impressed with the suggestion which is sometimes made, that many road accidents are preventable in the sense that they are due to a detectable illness in the driver of the vehicle. Very few traffic accidents are in fact due to any kind of physical collapse or disease of the driver (apart from the question of alcohol). Those few accidents which can be shown to be due to a sudden physical collapse in the driver, as for example a heart attack, are cases in which, had the most distinguished medical man examined the driver an hour previously, he would have pronounced him entirely fit to drive. Medicine, even now unfortunately, is still unable to be as perfect and omniscient as we all would wish it to be.

More could be done by more efficient road works and traffic sign engineering; but all this costs money. I could not help being amused by a copy which was sent to me of a road sign in Texas. It read: 'Drive damn careful. Dangerous coroner ahead".

As is well known, a favourite means of suicide in recent years has been by an overdoese of barbiturates, or sleeping tablets obtained on a prescription for the patient from the patient's doctor. I have always had the uneasy feeling that these drugs were too readily prescribed, and too easily obtained. Now, with the development and manufacture of other and safer hypnotic and sedative drugs, barbiturates are prescribed less. In a similar way the use of natural gas has tended to make less available domestic coal gas as a vehicle for suicide.

Over the years, with the active commercial promotion of them by the drug firms, more and more proprietary drugs have come on to the market, and have become available either on a doctor's prescription or by, in some cases, direct sale to the public. The public have come to believe that no consultation with a doctor can be complete without the patient emerging with that mystic piece of paper – the prescription. The public sees this as their "right"; have they not, they say, helped to pay for it? It takes a doctor of unusual integrity and honesty to tell a patient in many cases that no treatment is necessary, certainly no drug treatment. But, since he is in a competitive world, he has to consider the possibility of his patient transferring to the list of a more docile and more amenable practitioner.

The recent reorganisation of the National Health Service has so far turned out to be not the prescription for happiness and satisfaction that was expected. It may be surprising to many to learn that the National Health Service is the biggest employer in the country; some one million or so are employed in it. There has been a considerable proliferation of bureaucrats and administrators, who now considerably outnumber the doctors. I am one of those who retain the old-fashioned belief that the most important person in the National Health Service ought to be the patient, and that the patient's welfare should be paramount and above all else.

Regrettably, this is not always the case; some of the malaise of the Health Service stems, at least in part, from the bureaucracy and over-administration that is endemic in it. Some doctors have found so much of their time being required for sitting on various committees that they have less time to care for their patients than should be the case.

It was some years ago that I met Mr. Edgar Borrow, a remarkable man. Mr. Borrow, having spent a lifetime in dairy and agricultural pursuits, became very interested in the fluoride controversy. I do not need to say a great deal about the general aspects of this, because these, I think are fairly well known.

It is recognised by all authoritative opinion that the administration of fluoride in suitable dosage can radically diminish that scourge of our age – dental caries or dental decay: something which involves the state in vast expenditure in sick pay, loss of earnings, and loss of production; and further something which produces much human misery and suffering.

It is known that the administration of fluoride is really only effective when given during the period of the growing and erupting tooth, that is until the age of fourteen years. Giving fluoride to adults with already diseased teeth is of no practical value.

As is well known, the official policy of attempting to put fluoride into the general drinking water has provoked a good deal of opposition; cries of "mass medication" and loss of liberty have gone up, and much protest has been evinced. I take no sides in this controversy; but at least it is understandable.

Mr. Borrow reasoned that if fluoride, in the right dose, were given to school children in school milk or school meals (and then only to those children whose parents consented) the arguments of the anti-fluoride campaign would be sensibly met. He therefore founded and endowed the Borrow Dental Milk Foundation, a charitable foundation, with this as one of its objects. He has recruited a number of distinguished scientists, who are aiding him with research in his most laudable objectives. I may mention, among many others, Professor Hugh Sinclair of Oxford, Dr. Ziegler, of Winthertur in Switzerland, and Professor Leali in Milan. In fact projects – such as suggested by the Borrow Foundation – have already been carried out with children in the United States, Switzerland and Japan. All of these carefully researched and documented projects have shown a marked reduction in the number of carious teeth in the children who have taken fluoride, as compared with control groups of non-fluoridated children.

It has always seemed to me that Mr. Barrow's proposals are so logical, and so completely meet the opposition of the anti-fluoride (drinking water) lobby that it is surprising that official policy in Great Britain (first evolved by Mr. Enoch Powell, then Minister of Health a number of years ago) has remained firmly fixed to "fluoride in drinking water". I have been able – and was very glad to do so – to give Mr. Borrow what assistance I could with his proposals and the workings of the Foundation. He is an unusual man with a strong dedication to the cause which he has so generously and rightly supported. I wish him and the Foundation well in the future. By a curious coincidence, my son-in-law, Dr. John Faccini is a doctor and a dentist, who did much work and a subsequent thesis at King's College, Cambridge on the effect of fluoride on bone.

Chapter 3

Euthanasia: the Right to Die

One of the questions that has interested me has been the question of euthanasia – that is, the practice of terminating deliberately the lives of patients afflicted with incurable disease, at the patient's request. I have no very strong views on this subject one way or the other. But even if one were basically in favour of such a practice in appropriate cases, it seems to me that there would be considerable difficulty legally in making the practice free from malpractice and in providing adequate safeguards. But I think it right and worthwhile to set out here some observations on this subject whilst not, I think, putting forward any vehement views on one side or the other.

Over a hundred years ago it was written:

> "Thou shalt not kill, but needst not strive
> Officiously to keep alive".

It was Arthur Hugh Clough who wrote these words, and he could hardly have put it better. I merely quote what he wrote, but I am not sure that his tongue may not have been somewhat in his cheek when he wrote it.

The word "euthanasia" is derived from the Greek – meaning a good death – that is to say a comfortable, easy death such as we would all wish when the time comes. The cases under consideration are those tragic cases in which death alone can bring relief and an end to suffering.

The Concise Oxford English Dictionary defines euthanasia as "gentle and easy death; the bringing about of this, especially in cases of incurable and painful disease". Most thinking on this subject has been directed towards legalising voluntary euthanasia – terminating life on the written, formally and duly witnessed request by the patient that this should be done; this presupposes that the patient's mind is clear, and that he understands what he is doing, and what he is requesting. The position would be quite otherwise in what may be called compulsory euthanasia, some of the advocates of which would give legal sanction to the "mercy killing" of the congenitally mental defectives, the helpless and hopeless senile dements, the patients with permanent brain damage, and perhaps even such tragic cases as the thalidomide children. It is certain that Parliament would never approve compulsory euthanasia – or any such act without the consent of the patient. Certainly this will not be done before voluntary euthanasia is approved, and this is not yet the case. Some might see any such proposal without the request of the patient as the thin end of the wedge, with sinister overtones of Hitler's Germany.

On the battlefield, it has not been unknown for a gravely wounded soldier to request a comrade to dispatch him, and this has been done.

There have been several attempts to put on the Statute Book an Act permitting voluntary euthanasia; it may be that public opinion is not yet ready for such a step, and so far they have all failed.

It is urged that anybody who is suffering from an incurable condition should have the right to ask for his life to be ended in a peaceful and dignified way rather than to suffer constant pain, and face what has become nothing but a distressing, purposeless, or irrational existence. It is suggested that the old, the infirm, and the chronically diseased are, by their very nature and situation, not in a position to press a vigorous campaign for a change in the law; and for the same reason it could be argued in the opposite sense that those patients who might be thought to be suitable cases for euthanasia are precisely those who are not in a fit mental condition to make the written voluntary request for it which the last Bill in Parliament suggested.

The attitude of most of us towards death is conditioned by a number of things – by religious teaching, by a sense perhaps of what is the conventional attitude towards it, by sentiment, and by the very fear of it. Others accept that it need not necessarily be an enemy to be feared, but may indeed, in certain circumstances, come as a friend.

All of us will have the utmost sympathy with those who seek a way, within the law, to bring a merciful and earlier release to those who are racked with the pain and distress of incurable disease. It is said, with considerable force, that it is the quality of life that matters, and not its length. In other words, say the advocates of euthanasia, WHAT is being kept alive? In 1936 a Bill was moved, without success, and again in 1950 in the House of Lords on a motion – again without result.

Since then Parliament has made two significant changes in the law, which some may see as progressive, and some as the reverse. But they are changes which are notable. By the Suicide Act of 1961, it was enacted that suicide was no longer a crime; formerly suicide was a crime, indeed a felony – *felo de se*. Secondly, the passing of the Abortion Act has made it possible in a wide range of circumstances the legal destruction of the living foetus. Many people see in these new laws a more liberal approach towards the freedom of the individual; the State has, by implication, recognised the right of individuals to take their own lives, and the right to take the life of the living foetus in the womb. Accordingly it was felt that the climate might be favourable to another change in the law, and in March, 1969, the Voluntary Euthanasia Bill was read and debated in the House of Lords.

The Bill proposed the "painless inducement of death". It would have been lawful for a person to ask for this, and lawful for a physician to administer euthanasia to a patient who had made the appropriate declaration in writing. The patient must have reached the age of majority, and two physicians (one of whom must have been of consultant status) would have certified in writing that the patient was suffering from an irremediable condition. The cases provided for were described as "serious physical illness thought to be incurable, and expected to cause severe distress and render incapable of rational existence".

It may be that, sooner or later, society will re-adjust its attitude towards death and towards voluntary euthanasia, but the House of Lords in 1969 rejected the Bill and its proposals. The vote against the Bill was undoubtedly swayed by the opinions of the medical peers and of the bishops.

It is possible to see certain practical difficulties if ever voluntary euthanasia became legal, in the sense which the Bill envisaged. Who would perform the act of euthanasia? (Clearly, no doctor whose religious or other objections were against the measure would be expected to take part in it.) How would it be done? Would it be available as part of the National Health Service? Would it then, as has been experienced under the Abortion Act, because of the varying attitudes of doctors, be very much easier in some districts than others to obtain this service? These are all serious questions which were left unanswered in the Bill as it was introduced in the House of Lords. It may even be permissible to try to envisage the occasion when the appropriate official, be he doctor or otherwise, calls at the house of the patient on his unusual mission. (The Bill permitted the "authorised hospital doctor" to delegate his administration of euthanasia to a nurse.) Many would find this situation – the visit of the "euthanasia man" – utterly repugnant.

In a different sense, but related to these questions, are the problems presented by transplant operations. In the case of a young adult with irrecoverable brain damage following an accident, who is being kept alive only by an artificial breathing machine, can the State legalise the turning off of the machine so that the organs may be given to others? And if so, who is to turn the machine off, and who is to give the order to do so? These are questions about which the present law is quite unclear, and in which the practice of doctors may vary very much.

Physicians of great experience of patients of the kind in which voluntary euthanasia might be thought to be appropriate have said that in fact they have never been requested by patients that their lives should be ended; they add, however, that they have often been under pressure by the patient's relatives to do precisely this, and one must always remember that there are sometimes unscrupulous relatives (and occasionally unscrupulous doctors).

Several years ago, a hospital consultant posted a notice recommending his staff to withold resuscitation from certain groups of seriously ill people. This provoked considerable comment, but there was obviously much sympathy with the view that some people should be allowed to die peacefully without heroic attempts at revival being made. The opposite policy, it is argued, would result in the abler members of the community devoting their lives to preserving the existence of the decrepit. Since the advent of antibiotics the fatal pneumonia which used to be described as the "old man's friend" has ceased to remove the aged from the cares of their existence. Some feel that the risk to us all is not of dying, but of living too long. Obviously hospitals are never going to be able to provide all the beds, all the kidney machines, all the transplants, and all the intensive care units which would be required to keep alive a population consisting of more and more aged persons; nor, apparently are the politicians prepared to spend so great a part of the national income on projects of this kind. Such facilities will be granted to some, but not to others. The burden of these decisions will inevitably fall upon the shoulders of doctors.

Cancer is frequently mentioned as an example of the class of case of incurable disease in which euthanasia would be appropriate. But many thousands of these patients are treated, recover, enjoy life, and eventually die of something else. In medical science what is incurable this year may become curable next year. But many cancer patients do suffer great pain, and die in agony and misery.

There is a popular belief in such cases that in practice the doctor "helps the patient over the last hurdle". The good doctor, it is said, knows the difference between prolonging life and prolonging the act of dying. Certainly it is true that in a condition of ever-increasing pain it will be necessary to administer larger and larger doses of pain-killing and sedative drugs, even though it will be known that in doing so the patient's life may be shortened. Is there a difference between shortening a life and actively terminating it? Most doctors will maintain that there is such a difference. We, as patients, would perhaps hope, if ever we found ourselves in that situation, that our doctor would treat us in this humane and compassionate way; but one might have to be "lucky" in one's doctor, and there is no guarantee, from the patient's point of view, that this would happen. But in many distressing and incurable conditions pain itself may not be a symptom at all, or only a very insignificant one; and in these cases even the final merciful release of increasing doses of drugs cannot reasonably be expected.

No country in the world, it is believed, has yet legalised euthanasia, and both the World Medical Association and the British Medical Association are not in favour of it. A recent case of a hopelessly incurable child in the United States appears to have resulted in the court giving the child's parents the right to authorise the turning off of the breathing machine; but it appears that this decision of the court is under appeal, and the ultimate result is uncertain. Doctors are not sympathetic to a change in the law; nor would they welcome such a law which installed some doctors in the new and macabre role of terminators of life; certainly there would be no doctors volunteering for this post. In the 1950 debate in the House of Lords the late and distinguished Lord Horder said: "I hope that the decision will not rest with our profession. Some of our critics might advance the view that we already kill enough people".

But is this attitude on the part of doctors perhaps somewhat illogical? They are, in effect, saying that they have no objection to euthanasia so long as they administer it themselves in the humane way which results from the care of terminal patients with increasingly large doses of drugs, but that they would object to doing it on behalf of society. But is it fair to them that doctors should act on their professional judgment regardless of the criminal law? A doctor should not have to face the possible risk of criminal prosecution, or of blackmail, simply because he does what he believes to be right, and in the best interests of a distressed and incurable patient. It may be equally unfair to the patient who believes that he has a right to die before he has lost all human dignity, if his doctor happens to have religious or conscientious scruples which oblige him to let his patient's illness take its natural course. Also, the possibilities of a merciful release might well depend on a patient's means, or whether he was in a public ward or a private nursing home.

The complex problems involved in this highly sensitive area are legal, ethical, medical and religious; and what remains to be seen is whether all these difficulties can be resolved, and safely codified in an Act of Parliament. Although the recent attempt to do so has, for the moment failed, it seems certain that we shall inevitably have to consider these questions again in the future and, perhaps, re-orientate our conventional attitudes towards life and death. Society will have to make up its mind.

Finally, I am reminded of some observations by Lord Hill in a recent book of his reminiscences after a lifetime of distinguished public service.

I do not claim to remember his exact words, but he refers to the frequently expressed view that to do nothing in retirement is a sure recipe for physical and mental deterioration. "Keep working", he says is the text of these gloomy prophets.

He comments that if in retirement he decides to "do damn-all", that can be done with dignity and delight and that, perhaps with some minor changes, is just what he will propose to do in due course. I am bound to say that, although without his eminent qualifications, this is a view with which I have much sympathy.

Index